Comments on other *Amazing Stories* from readers & reviewers

"Tightly written volumes filled with lots of wit and humour about famous and infamous Canadians."

Eric Shackleton, *The Globe and Mail*

"The heightened sense of drama and intrigue, combined with a good dose of human interest is what sets Amazing Stories *apart."*

Pamela Klaffke, *Calgary Herald*

"This is popular history as it should be...For this price, buy two and give one to a friend."

Terry Cook, a reader from Ottawa, on **Rebel Women**

"Glasner creates the moment of the explosion itself in graphic detail...she builds detail upon gruesome detail to create a convincingly authentic picture."

Peggy McKinnon, *The Sunday Herald,* on **The Halifax Explosion**

"It was wonderful...I found I could not put it down. I was sorry when it was completed."

Dorothy F. from Manitoba on **Marie-Anne Lagimodière**

"Stories are rich in description, and bristle with a clever, stylish realness."

Mark Weber, *Central Alberta Advisor,* on **Ghost Town Stories II**

"A compelling read. Bertin...has selected only the most intriguing tales, which she narrates with a wealth of detail."

Joyce Glasner, *New Brunswick Reader,* on **Strange Events**

"The resulting book is one readers will want to share with all the women in their lives."

Lynn Martel, *Rocky Mountain Outlook,* on **Women Explorers**

DISASTER AT DIEPPE

DISASTER AT DIEPPE

The biggest catastrophe in Canadian military history

Jim Lotz

HISTORY

James Lorimer & Company Ltd., Publishers
Toronto

James Lorimer & Company Ltd., Publishers acknowledges the support of the Ontario Arts Council. We acknowledge the financial support of the Government of Canada through the Canada Book Fund for our publishing activities. We acknowledge the support of the Canada Council for the Arts which last year invested $24.3 million in writing and publishing throughout Canada. We acknowledge the Government of Ontario through the Ontario Media Development Corporation's Ontario Book Initiative.

ONTARIO ARTS COUNCIL
CONSEIL DES ARTS DE L'ONTARIO

Canada Council
for the Arts

Cover image: Library and Archives Canada, C-014160.

Library and Archives Canada Cataloguing in Publication

Lotz, Jim, 1929-
Disaster at Dieppe : the biggest catastrophe in Canadian military history / Jim Lotz.

(Amazing stories)
Includes bibliographical references and index.
Issued also in an electronic format.
ISBN 978-1-4594-0172-3

1. Dieppe Raid, 1942. 2. Canada--Armed Forces--History--World War, 1939-1945. 3. World War, 1939-1945--Campaigns--France. I. Title. II. Series: Amazing stories (Toronto, Ont.)

D756.5.D5L68 2012   940.54'21425   C2012-903688-9

James Lorimer & Company Ltd., Publishers
317 Adelaide Street West, Suite 1002
Toronto, ON, Canada
M5V 1P9
www.lorimer.ca

Printed and bound in Canada

Contents

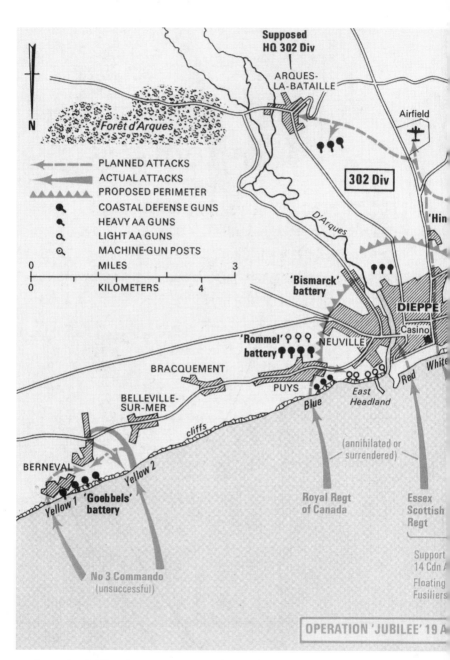

Operation Jubilee, August 19, 1942, 2nd Canadian Division

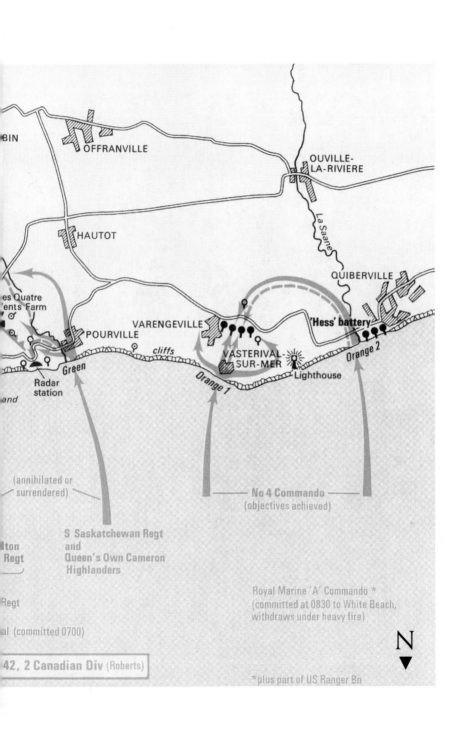

OFFRANVILLE

BIN

OUVILLE-
LA-RIVIERE

HAUTOT

La Saane

QUIBERVILLE

es Quatre
ents Farm

VARENGEVILLE

'Hess' battery

POURVILLE

cliffs

VASTERIVAL-
SUR-MER

Orange 2

Orange 1

Green

Lighthouse

Radar
station

and

(annihilated or
surrendered)

No 4 Commando
(objectives achieved)

ton
Regt

S Saskatchewan Regt
and
Queen's Own Cameron
Highlanders

Regt

Royal Marine 'A' Commando *
(committed at 0830 to White Beach,
withdraws under heavy fire)

al (committed 0700)

42, 2 Canadian Div (Roberts)

*plus part of US Ranger Bn

N
▼

Chapter 1
The Reason Why

"Some one had blunder'd:
Theirs not to make reply,
Theirs not to reason why,
Theirs but to do and die"
　　　　—Tennyson, "The Charge
　　　　　　of the Light Brigade"

In a speech in London on November 10, 1942, Prime Minister Winston Churchill reviewed the progress of the war. The tide had turned, the Allies were finally winning battles. But, as he put it: "Now this is not the end. It is not the beginning of the end. But it is, perhaps, the end of the beginning."

For Bob Prouse and three thousand of his Canadian comrades, that year marked the end of their war. Prouse,

Bodies of soldiers lying among damaged landing craft and Churchill tanks of the Calgary Regiment following Operation Jubilee, August 19, 1942.

a member of the Canadian Provost Corps, had been bored stiff waiting in England to go into action. He jumped at the opportunity to take part in "a little manoeuvre coming up," expecting to direct traffic or look after German prisoners.

At noon on August 19, 1942, Prouse, wounded in the leg, lay on the beach at the French coastal port of Dieppe under a wrecked landing craft. Nearby sprawled a dead infantryman. Machine guns and mortars continued their killing work on the beach while Prouse rescued a soldier from being run over by a Canadian tank and saw another soldier crushed under its treads.

Prouse felt no fear, only a sense of detachment.

He became one of almost 2,000 prisoners captured

by the Germans in one of the worst military disasters in Canadian history.

The reasons for the attack on Dieppe, and its tragic failure, still generate controversy today. Churchill, the aggressive war leader, favoured a major assault on enemy-held territory to boost the morale of the British people. He assigned Lord Louis Mountbatten, a national hero and head of Combined Operations, to organize it. Josef Stalin, leader of the embattled Soviet Union, continually pressed the British and Americans to invade Europe as his armies retreated before the German onslaught on Russia. The Americans, who had entered the war in December 1941, also wanted to go on the attack.

When the idea of a large-scale raid on the French coast arose in the spring of 1942, General Harry Crerar, commander of the First Canadian Corps, pressed for his soldiers to take part in it. They had been training for two years and were considered ready for action.

The American writer I. F. Stone observed: "[The] most interesting bit of fact I have picked up...is that the Canadians have spoken up vigorously for an early second front at official military discussions. This may explain why Dieppe was so predominantly a Canadian affair. It looks as though the British said, 'Well, if you're anxious for a second front, go and try one.'"

The Second Canadian Infantry Division, commanded by Major General John Hamilton ("Ham") Roberts, and tanks from the First Canadian Armoured Division, a total of just over 5,000 men, would make up most of the attacking force.

Operation Rutter, mounted in early July, was cancelled because of bad weather and the attack on France, codenamed Operation Jubilee, was remounted for August 19. It would be, in the words of a public relations officer, "The biggest Canadian Army story that has broken so far in this war." And so it proved to be.

The Plan of Attack

Dieppe, known as "Deepy" by the soldiers, lay in a cleft on the French coast, about 100 kilometres from England. A pleasant tourist spot, the town was known as "The Poor Man's Monte Carlo" and offered the nearest beach to Paris. A casino anchored the western end of a long promenade that lay behind a seawall fronting the beach. Intelligence reports claimed that the port was lightly defended by poor-quality German troops. They did not mention that Dieppe's beaches consisted of shale and pebbles the size of baseballs that would trip soldiers, cripple tanks, and turn into missiles when hit by mortar bombs. Nor did they mention that the cliffs that hemmed in Dieppe had been hollowed out and turned into gun emplacements that covered the beach and the sea approaches to them.

The misleading intelligence reports inspired overconfidence in those planning the raid. In this instance, as in many aspects of Operation Jubilee, someone had blundered.

Among other things, the tactical goals of the raid—in

Personnel of the Royal Canadian Army Medical Corps treating "casualties" during the final rehearsal for Operation Jubilee, the raid on Dieppe. England, August 1942.

contrast to the grandiose strategic ones—were vague. Major General Roberts outlined them on the command ship, HMS *Calpe,* to Quentin Reynolds, an American war correspondent: "We want, if possible, to destroy shipping in the harbour, grab a radio direction finder, destroy the torpedo factory...the raid will show the Hun that he can't relax his vigilance anywhere on the coastline; that he must, in fact, strengthen his defences. He can only do that by withdrawing troops, planes, and guns from Russia."

The British navy refused to risk any of its large warships in the operation. The Royal Air Force would not commit heavy bombers to soften up the targets before the attack. The reason for this decision was humanitarian (the fear of killing French civilians) and tactical (rubble created by heavy bombardment would hinder tank action).

The plan called for two teams of British commandos to take out the gun batteries on the headlands overlooking Dieppe. To the east, on Blue Beach, the Royal Regiment of Canada and three platoons from the Black Watch of Canada would take the heights and swing west in a pincer movement around Dieppe. To the west, on Green Beach, the South Saskatchewan Regiment and the Queen's Own Cameron Highlanders would move inland and link up with the Royals. They would hold the line against enemy attacks while the Royal Hamilton Light Infantry (the Rileys) and the Essex Scottish would land on White and Red Beaches supported by tanks of the Calgary Regiment. They were expected to enter Dieppe, blow up the telephone exchange, the torpedo factory, and anything else of use to the enemy. Les Fusiliers Mont-Royal (FMR) and a unit of Royal Marine Commandos, serving as a floating reserve, would land later and contribute to the general mayhem.

After a few hours, the Canadian soldiers would retreat to the beaches to be picked up by the Royal Navy and head back to England.

Things did not quite work out this way; no plan survives first contact with the enemy.

Chapter 2
The First Assaults

"...it seems to have a reasonable chance of success."

—General Andrew McNaughton,
Commander, First Canadian Army

In a schoolhouse in Lansing, Sussex, Lieutenant Colonel Dollard Menard, commander of the FMR, prepared his troops: "*Mes gars, ca y'est.*" (This is it, lads.) Father Sabourin then offered Holy Communion to the 619 men of the battalion. Menard recalled one officer who for years had not been to church to take communion and who was "among the first to be killed the next morning." Major Paul Savoy, at forty considered too old for combat, had pleaded with Menard to be allowed to go with the men. The commander told him:

"I don't want to see you again until after we [have] sailed." Savoy also died on the beach at Dieppe.

The Germans may not have been forewarned of the attack, but they were definitely on the alert because of weather and tide conditions. The commander of the German troops at Dieppe, Colonel General Conrad Haase, had issued an Order of the Day: *The information in our hands makes it clear that the Anglo-Americans will be forced...by the wretched predicament of the Russians to undertake some operations in the West in the near future.* Placing his men on the alert, Haase added, "The troops must grasp the fact that when it happens it will be a very sticky business."

While the bulk of the attacking force of approximately 6,000 consisted of Canadian troops, approximately 400 British commandos, American Rangers, and a small contingent of Free French soldiers also took part in Operation Jubilee.

As an armada of 237 ships—destroyers, gunboats, flak (anti-aircraft) ships, and landing craft—crept across the English Channel, it ran into a German coastal convoy of three torpedo boats (E-boats) escorting five motor ships also heading for Dieppe. At precisely 0347 hours on the morning of August 19, a star shell burst above the ships, turning night briefly into day, and the shooting started. Machine-gun bullets ripped into the thin armour of British motor torpedo boats. Landing craft broke formation, their low profiles making them difficult to see and hit. A Royal Navy gunboat engaged the enemy which quickly silenced its guns, leaving their crews dead and wounded. A shell hit the boiler room, crippling the British vessel and forcing it to stop. Suddenly the shooting ceased. The German convoy proceeded on its way, as sailors on the British ships scrambled to repair damage and treat the wounded.

Some of the damaged ships and landing craft, including those carrying two-thirds of No. 3 Commando and some of the Royals, headed back to England. The remainder of the armada continued on through a minefield. Norm Bowen of the Royal Canadian Navy, coxswain of one of the landing craft, recalled seeing a Dan buoy, asking: "'What the hell is that?' and was told, 'That's the beginning of the minefield.' So I kept on going a little further and about an hour later I said, 'There's another Dan buoy, what's that?' [and was told] 'That's the end of the minefield.' We had a shallow enough draft to go right over the top of [the mines]." Landing Craft Personnel (LCP) 15 had flanked the German ships, escaped through fierce tracer fire, and sailed towards Yellow Beach. On board were twenty members of No. 3 Commando, the remnant of the force assigned to silence the guns at Berneval on the Eastern Headland overlooking Dieppe.

The Commandos Attack

Led by Major Peter Young, the men on LCP 15 leapt ashore, raced up the undefended beach and made for a gully choked

Canadian dead litter the Dieppe beach among ruined and abandoned tanks.

with barbed wire. Climbing up the side of it, the Commandos reached the top of the chalk cliff and dashed towards the enemy guns. Young knew that his force was too weak to attack them, but he devised a plan to keep them from firing on the Allied fleet. Reaching the Berneval battery, his men hunkered down in a cornfield. Armed only with Tommy and Bren guns, they kept up a steady fire on the German gunners. When the Germans turned their powerful weapons on their attackers, the blast almost lifted them from their positions as the shells whistled over their heads. Their ammunition running low, the Commandos reached the gully, swarmed down it, dashed across the beach, and jumped aboard the waiting landing craft. A few of them had been wounded, but none killed. For two vital hours, they had kept the heavy guns of the Berneval battery from wreaking havoc among the British ships.

Another force of Commandos that included six Rangers (their American equivalent) also landed to take out the guns at Berneval. Approaching the beach as first light broke, they encountered two machine guns that poured fire on them as they left the landing craft. Lieutenant (Lt.) Edwin Loustalot charged towards one of them and became the first American soldier to die in the European theatre. A Commando took out the other German gun. The surviving attackers headed for a gully, huddling there while Germans on the cliff poured fire down on them. At 1000 hours they attacked, overwhelming the Commandos, taking eighty-two of them prisoner.

Things went better to the west as Lieutenant Colonel Lord Lovat's No. 4 Commando came ashore. He ordered his men to attack the six guns at Varengeville "at the greatest possible risk." And they did. One of them reported later: "It was a piece of cake. We got close to them before they even knew we were there."

At 0450 hours, precisely on time, and with no opposition, Lovat's force of 245 Commandos, six Rangers, and two Free French Commandos landed on Yellow Beach. Finding a pathway up the cliff face blocked with barbed wire, they blew it open, climbed up, and made for the German battery as its huge guns opened fire on the fleet lying off Dieppe. An anti-tank gunner put a heavy machine gun on a tower out of action, while snipers killed members of the battery crew.

A cannon-firing Hurricane fighter roared in from above, shooting up the enemy position. A huge explosion rocked the battery: shells and explosive charges near the guns had been hit. As Hurricanes strafed the Germans, the Commandos charged the enemy with fixed bayonets. They wiped out 112 members of the gun crew and captured four survivors. Spiking and blowing up the guns, the Commandos set fire to all the buildings of the battery. Then they held their traditional ceremony, placing their dead on a pyre, setting fire to it, raising the Union Jack, saluting it, and retreating to the beach. A signal went out, saying, "Battery demolished at 0650 hours." No. 4 Commando's casualties totalled 46 killed, wounded, and missing.

The attack on the Varengeville battery showed what could be done by experienced, well-trained troops under a formidable leader attacking a specific target. Unfortunately, unlike these troops, Canada's soldiers, although well-trained, had no experience in battle. They would pay dearly for this lack of experience when they landed on the beaches of Dieppe.

Chapter 3
Blue Beach

"All in all, it would have been difficult to discover, anywhere on the coast of Europe, a less favourable area for an assault landing."
—Brereton Greenhous, *Dieppe, Dieppe*

War correspondent Quentin Reynolds told of a soldier returning from the beaches, gasping out as he was carried aboard HMS *Calpe*: "'How did I get out? We touched down and stepped ashore, and machine guns came from both sides, everyone was hit—except me. They kept shooting at us. They were all killed except me. They never hit me.'" Reynolds added: "Then he died."

The plan called for the Royal Regiment of Canada (the Royals) and 110 soldiers of the Black Watch of Canada to land on Blue Beach, about a kilometre east of Dieppe, and ascend the cliffs above it. They would knock out an anti-aircraft battery there, capture a holiday camp the Germans had turned into a barracks, and take the Bismarck battery on the Eastern Headland to prevent it firing on the beaches where the Rileys and the Essex Scottish would land. Members of the Royal Canadian Artillery would help the Royals to capture the battery and turn its weapons on the enemy. The invaders would then make contact with the Essex Scottish who were supposed to take over Dieppe. A detachment of the Royal Canadian Engineers would blow up the gasworks. The Black Watch would protect the flanks of the Royals.

Canadian war correspondent Ross Munro accompanied the Royals into battle. Eating with the regiment's officers in the wardroom, he reported they were "in good spirits. Looking around the table you would never have thought they were facing the biggest test of their lives." For many of the officers, this would be their last meal. Of the 550 members of the Royals who took part in Operation Jubilee, only 65 would return to England, and all but 33 of them wounded.

Blue Beach at Puits (also known as Puys) stretched for 200 metres below the overhanging cliffs cut by a narrow valley. At its base, a hundred-metre-long and three-metre-high seawall, topped with spiked concertina wire, barred access. A footpath wound up the gorge and two flights of steps led down to the beach.

Canadian troops embarking in landing craft during a training exercise before the raid on Dieppe, France, circa August 1942.

The Landing

The seven landing craft carrying the Royals approached Blue Beach in darkness through geysers of water created by shells and mortar bombs. On the cliffs, a small detachment of German infantry trained their guns on the landing site below them. Ross Munro wrote: "We bumped on the beach and down went the ramp and out poured the first infantrymen. They plunged into about two feet of water and machine-gun bullets laced into them. Bodies piled up on the ramp. Some staggered to the beach and fell. Bullets were splattering into the boat itself, wounding and killing our men."

Major Schofield, commander of the first of three waves of attacks, was wounded and died as he left the ramp. The slaughter accelerated as first light dawned. Soldiers dashed for the seawall, which offered scant protection. A machine gun on the eastern slope of the gully fired. A soldier stood up, screaming, and fired a Bren gun at it. With his ammunition exhausted, he continued screaming at the enemy until he was cut down. Lieutenant Wedd's platoon reached the seawall as a pillbox opened up on them. Scrambling to it under a hail of bullets, the officer pushed a grenade through the firing slit, killing the gunners.

Peering over the bow of the landing craft, Munro saw sixty to seventy Royals lying dead near the seawall: "They had been cut down before they had a chance to fire a shot." Near him, a young soldier, wounded in the arm, had made several attempts to rush to the beach. Lunging forward, he collapsed as red-white tracer slashed open his stomach. Crying in anguish on the blood-stained deck, "Christ, we gotta beat them, we gotta beat them," he died. An officer, hit in the head, fell over Munro's legs while nearby a sailor with a gash in his throat gasped out his life.

Another officer reported: "As I left the assault craft I saw perhaps a hundred dead men." More soldiers reached the seawall and took cover there. Sgt. Legate noted that, if you moved a metre from it, "you got it."

The Royals were trapped. The scaling ladders to climb

the cliffs had been left on the landing craft. One troop of German gunners fired 550 rounds at the ships, crippling most of them. The one carrying Munro did manage to leave the beach with its cargo of dead and wounded soldiers. He wrote: "On no other front have I witnessed such a carnage."

The members of Force Edward, made up mainly of members of the Black Watch, landed under a cliff where German machine guns could not reach them. Four men were killed and eight wounded before the rest surrendered.

Corporal Ellis Goes It Alone

Cpl. L. G. Ellis, a sniper, emerged unscathed from a landing craft, ran across the beach and started up a double flight of steps at the western end of the seawall. Moving through a gap blown in the wire, he dismantled booby traps, took cover in a depression, and moved up to the top of the cliff. Looking for targets, he saw a pillbox at which his comrades were shooting. The machine gunner, however, was not inside it—he had concealed himself in nearby bushes. Taking aim at a small exposed part of the hidden man's face, Ellis killed him.

Then he slid down the gully towards the beach. On the way he grabbed a wounded Royal and dragged him towards the beach. Suddenly an explosion blasted his face and filled his arms and legs with shrapnel. The man Ellis was rescuing had triggered a booby trap that killed him. Somehow, still under fire, the corporal reached the beach. With bullets whizzing by him and hitting the pebbles, he calmly undressed and entered the corpse-crowded sea. Avoiding sniper fire by feigning death, and sinking out of sight in the water, Ellis stripped life jackets off two dead soldiers. A strong swimmer, his strength had begun to ebb just as Sgt. Legate pulled him out of the water into a rowboat. In the hour that he spent behind enemy lines, the corporal had not seen a single German except the machine gunner he killed.

A handful of Royals reached the top of the cliffs.

Major Catto realized he had no hope of survival on the beach. Accompanied by a sergeant, he cut a hole in the wire blocking the gully. Twenty soldiers followed them as they rushed upwards. At the clifftop, the small band attacked a fortified house and dealt with six machine gunners. Encountering heavy fire, Catto and his men hunkered down, powerless to act as a six-gun 88-mm battery came under attack by Hurricane fighters. Finding the road to Dieppe patrolled and guarded by machine guns, the Canadians found refuge in a small wood and eventually surrendered to a German patrol at 1635 hours.

Leaving Blue Beach

The enemy fire on the soldiers on the beach intensified as the morning drew on, with mortar bombs and heavy artillery shells turning Blue Beach into a charnel house. The Germans on the cliffs dropped grenades on the Canadians. If they tried

German officers standing on Dieppe beach among Canadian dead and wounded.

to dodge the grenades, snipers shot them. A sergeant and three soldiers found a mortar, set it up, and fired three rounds before being wiped out. Two Royal Navy armed support craft engaged enemy positions for two hours before being driven off by coastal artillery, their gun crews all dead or wounded. HMS *Garth*, sailing at full speed along the shore, destroyed enemy positions on the clifftop. Its ammunition expended, the badly damaged destroyer picked up survivors from the water and set course for England.

Fifty soldiers rushed to the last assault boat to touch down, overwhelming it. The captain could not raise the ramp. As the overloaded boat backed away from the shore, the captain screamed at the soldiers to evacuate it. A sniper killed him. Shells burst nearby. The landing craft filled with water and turned turtle. Soldiers clung to its keel. Snipers picked them off, one by one. Sgt. Legate swam into the Channel, spotted a rowboat floating idly by, climbed into it, and scanned the sea. The sergeant rescued three other soldiers, including the indomitable Cpl. Ellis, before a flak ship pulled them out of their craft. The skipper received orders to return to England. Before they reached him, he drove his boat to within 100 metres of the beach and picked up about ten more soldiers from the water. On Blue Beach, the dead, the wounded, and the living lay silent and immobile under the brilliant morning sun. As smoke drifted over them, a dirty white handkerchief attached to a rifle rose from the bodies.

The Royal Regiment of Canada had surrendered. At 0835 hours, a signal from Germany's 571 Infantry regiment reached General Haase: "Puits firmly in our hands; enemy has lost about 500 prisoners and dead." A German officer reported that some of his men vomited when they saw the carnage they had wrought on Blue Beach.

In his book on the Dieppe raid, Terence Robertson wrote: "No episode on that day...illustrates more tragically the fatuity of military predictions, the disastrous consequences of planning for one set of circumstances to the exclusion of others..."

Chapter 4
Green Beach

"What the hell is going on? Why won't
someone tell me?"

> —General Roberts, awaiting
> messages from Green Beach

Flight Sergeant Jack Nissenthal, a radar expert, landed with
the South Saskatchewans on Green Beach. Part of the invasion plan called for him to accompany them to the high
land on the eastern bank of the Scie river valley where they
could capture a radar station. Nissenthal was to supervise the
removal of significant bits to help the Allies determine how
advanced the Germans were in this field. Two soldiers accompanied the airman. If there was any possibility that Nissenthal
might be captured, they were to kill him.

Fortunately, he escaped unharmed from the raid.

The plan also called for the South Saskatchewans to secure Green Beach below Pourville, three kilometres west of Dieppe, "with minimum delay to enable the Camerons of Canada to pass through without opposition." The Camerons were then expected to advance inland to capture Quatre Vents Farm, a German strongpoint. One company was supposed to destroy a repair shop and machine gun position on the western slopes of the Scie river, which bisected Green Beach, while another cleared Pourville.

The South Saskatchewans, for their part, were expected to land on the eastern side of the Scie river, assault the high ground beyond it, take out enemy batteries, and capture the radar station. They were then to establish a perimeter around Dieppe and link up with the Essex Scottish coming from the east.

These objectives proved hopelessly unrealistic. Even before they began, No. 14 Platoon of the South Saskatchewans lost half its strength when a mishandled grenade exploded on HMS *Invicta*.

Led by Lt. Col. Cecil Merritt, the South Saskatchewans landed on Green Beach at 0552 hours, two minutes behind schedule and without a shot being fired at them. The beach, backed by a seawall and overlooked by cliffs, stretched for 600 metres. The air smelled of seaweed and salt, noted Wally Reyburn, a war correspondent who went ashore with the

South Saskatchewans. The soldiers dashed across the beach "like a herd of elephants charging across a field of walnuts," as one of them put it. Instead of landing to the east of the Scie river, most of the Canadians ended up on its western side. To reach their objectives, they would have to cross a bridge over the river. The wire at the foot of the cliffs proved impossible to cut. Someone noticed a section of the seawall where the wire had been replaced by a sandbagged blockhouse that had not fired on them, so the Canadians climbed the cliffs there and headed towards the bridge over the river Scie.

The Camerons Land

As the landing craft carrying the Camerons approached Green Beach, German gunners, now fully alert, enshrouded them with curtains of shell fire. Able Seaman (AB) Albert Kirby of the Royal Canadian Naval Volunteer Reserve (RCNVR) recalls the deafening noise of sailing though "a massive sea volcano as the rain of mortar fire descended upon the water in front of us." He saw a piper standing on a landing craft "playing away as though he was alone in a field of heather." Lt. Col. Alfred Gostling, commander of the Camerons, cheered his men on, pointing out the enemy positions firing on them. As he leapt ashore, the officer died with a bullet through his head. Major Law, the regiment's second-in-command, took over and led his men into Pourville.

Meanwhile, the South Saskatchewans also moved into the town and headed for the bridge over the Scie river. They

Entry of the 2nd Canadian Infantry Division into Dieppe, September 3, 1944.

set up battalion headquarters in the garage of an empty house until mortar shells made it untenable. Moving to a grassy square near the house, the party was hit by mortar fire that killed an officer and four German prisoners. Wally Reyburn noted how the French people "remained perfectly calm and showed not the slightest sign of panic." Before the operation, the Allies had sent messages to the people of Dieppe, telling them not to become involved in the fighting.

The Bridge over the Scie

The bridge over the Scie river became the site of some of the fiercest fighting of the Dieppe raid. More a causeway than a bridge, it had no balustrades and was covered by guns in a huge concrete fortress. The Germans had dammed the river, turning its eastern outlet into a three-metre-deep lake. Machine guns and snipers opened up on the first Canadians to reach the bridge. Nissenthal, waiting to cross to reach the radar station, watched men of A Company of the South Saskatchewans die as they stormed the bridge, calling it: "A tragedy that had to be seen to be understood."

Captain Murray Osten of the same company led another charge across the bridge. Men died all around him, but he and a few others reached the far side of the bridge and found cover behind a road block. A pillbox on a hill raked them with machine-gun fire. Private Charles Sawden walked up to it, threw two grenades through the firing slits and killed the Germans inside. The South Saskatchewans advanced along the edge of the Scie through hidden pillboxes, gun pits, and sniper positions, killing the enemies inside, while suffering their own casualties. The Germans used smokeless ammunition, and changed their position constantly, making them difficult to locate. Here, as elsewhere, snipers picked off officers and non-commissioned officers (NCOs) to deprive the soldiers of leadership. Some of the South Saskatchewans who landed on the east bank of the Scie charged a light anti-aircraft battery firing on the Camerons, and killed every member of the gun crew with their bayonets. They were too few in number to capture the radar station, but they were able to cut cables leading to it.

Lt. Col. Merritt arrived from battalion headquarters and saw his men crouching by the side of the road leading to the bridge on which the dead lay, two deep.

"What was the problem?" he asked a soldier.

"This bridge is a hot spot, sir," the man replied. "We're trying to cross it."

Looking at the bridge, its surface gashed by shells and pitted by bullets, Merritt noticed a large grey house about 100 metres from the bridge's farthest end. If his men could reach it, they would have shelter from the enemy fire.

Merritt took off his helmet, wiped his sweaty brow, and addressed his men: "We're going to get across. Follow me. Don't bunch up together. Here we go." Erect, bareheaded, swinging his helmet on his wrist, the officer led his men across the bridge.

Reyburn recalled the scene in a CBC broadcast: "As I watched him lead his men through that thundering barrage, I felt a shiver run up and down my spine. I'd never seen anything like it."

Inspired by his example, troops dashed across the bridge. Only four died. Merritt shouted to the others: "See that! Hardly anyone got hit." He ran forward, forty soldiers at his heels, and led an attack on a pillbox, knocking it out, and taking three prisoners. Back at battalion headquarters, Merritt told his adjutant: "I've just bombed a pillbox. Try it sometime before breakfast. I recommend it for the appetite."

Clearing Pourville

Beyond the bridge over the Scie, Pourville became a battlefield as the South Saskatchewans cleared the Germans from it. Wally Reyburn recalled the wide main street of the town lined with shops, hotels, and houses with picket fences becoming the scene of burning buildings, decapitated trees, downed telegraph wires, discarded equipment, and the other detritus of war. Sgt. Howard Graham, Sten gun over his shoulder, battledress blouse filled with incendiary grenades, strolled down a street, intent on flushing out a sniper. He hurled the grenades into houses until the sniper emerged, clothes on fire, hands in the air. A machine gun on a cliffside fired down streets. Private Rogal knocked it out with an anti-tank rifle, and then provided covering fire for his comrades across the Scie.

The Canadians took fifty prisoners who had to be guarded, which sapped their fighting strength. A corporal noticed Germans in civilian clothes pointing out Canadian positions to snipers. When captured, they were shot. Other prisoners "got killed accidentally," as one soldier put it. In one house, three French women offered the visitors wine and biscuits while they fired at the enemy. "It sure was a good battle while it lasted—in that house," one soldier reported.

Under constant mortar fire, Merritt moved among the fighters, giving them encouragement. A party under Major Claude Orme headed for a large hotel overlooking the beach. Killing the sentries, they broke into the building, and discovered French and Belgian slave labourers constructing anti-invasion defences. They let them leave the hotel and go on their way.

Lt. Kempton led sixteen of his men in an attack on a German position. His platoon sergeant told what happened: "On nearing the objective, Mr. Kempton insisted on going ahead before allowing us to attack...Coming back, he reorganized the plan of attack and led the charge himself. The attack was successful due to his leadership and the determination of the men to follow him wherever he went."

Kempton searched for snipers on the flanks of his platoon as the Germans made an attempt to catch the Canadians in a pincer movement. He ordered his men to withdraw, covering them as they did so under smoke from a mortar. The Germans opened fire, wounding a Bren gunner and killing Kempton. The rest of his men escaped unscathed.

The Camerons Advance
While the South Saskatchewans roamed Pourville in search of Germans and fought at the bridge over the Scie, the Camerons moved inland. In two groups, they had landed

a half-hour late, under fire from the cliffs. The blockhouse that the South Saskatchewans had bypassed blew up, killing several soldiers. Some of the Camerons joined the fighting in Pourville while others advanced though woods into a field covered by machine guns. Taking out one of them, the Canadians moved left and reached a ridge overlooking the village of Hautot. Here they expected to rendezvous with the tanks of the Calgary Regiment, according to the plan. There was no sign of the tanks, but plenty of Germans in the land below the ridge. The Camerons attacked them as more poured out of the village and down the road from Pourville. A group under Major Law reached the trench system in front of Quatre Vents Farm, the deepest penetration into enemy territory achieved by the Canadians.

Offshore, HMS *Albrighton* fired ineffectively against targets its gunners could not see or locate. Two landing craft and a gunboat provided fire support for the Canadian troops until their guns jammed and their crews lay dead or wounded.

At 0945 hours, Merritt received the code word *Vanquish*, the order for his men and the Camerons to retire to the beach at 1100 hours to be picked up by the Royal Navy. The Camerons made a fighting retreat while the Germans stayed in their positions and fired on them, as German reinforcements occupied the high ground above Green Beach.

The South Saskatchewans and the Camerons formed a defensive perimeter to protect the troops as they swarmed down to the beach. Two hundred wounded men huddled behind the seawall. German fighters, machine guns blazing, swooped down on them.

Colonel Merritt's Last Stand

As the rescue boats arrived, Merritt directed that the wounded be loaded first. He told his men: "Don't run. Slope arms and march to the beach." Wally Reyburn, coming down the cliff, noticed a ladder leading to it, at the bottom of which lay a bundle of khaki-clad figures, soldiers who had been shot while descending it. He jumped down instead and landed safely. The war correspondent recalled again the smell of salt and seaweed, now mixed with blood, which assailed his nostrils as he waited to be rescued. Smoke and haze from burning buildings filled the air. The Germans concentrated their fire on the incoming boats as their aircraft bombed and strafed them. Between the safety of the cliff's edge and the shore lay 300 metres of pebbles and sand. Reyburn, when asked by Quentin Reynolds what it was like on the shore, replied: "Bloody awful," adding: "The last hour was the worst, just waiting for the boats to take us off. They came on the dot, but the tide was out and we had to run three hundred yards through machine-gun and mortar fire."

Reyburn rushed to a boat. It stuck. Soldiers pushed it away from the beach. Reyburn grabbed a rope hanging from the side of the boat. A bullet hit the man next to him in the head and he dropped into the blood-red sea. The boat began to sink. Reyburn jumped onto another landing craft. He told of the noise of explosions from bombs falling around the vessel: "As though you'd hit a giant glass with a giant tuning fork."

Reyburn's boat reached HMS *Calpe*. The shivering man was taken on board, led to the wardroom, and given a drink of brandy as the ship dodged dive bombers and shells.

Back on land, Merritt and Law commanded the rearguard. Merritt took a party of volunteers to knock out machine gunners firing on the escaping soldiers. Two destroyers bombarded the German positions and picked up men from the water as the tide rose. Seeing a soldier in danger of drowning, Merritt rushed to rescue him, taking a bullet in the shoulder. A Cameron pulled the officer to safety.

By 1100 hours, the rearguard of 180 men had done all it could to ensure that as many of their comrades as possible had left the beach.

Then the soldiers surrendered.

The South Saskatchewans and the Camerons went into battle 1,026 strong. Of these, 154 were killed, 269 wounded, and 256 captured.

Lt. Col. Merritt won the Victoria Cross (VC) for his bravery and leadership at the bridge over the river Scie and on the beach. Of the former action, he said: "There was nothing heroic about it. That was my regiment—and it was my job."

To boost civilian morale after the disaster at Dieppe, the Canadian government issued a poster with the headline: "Men of Valor. They fight for you." A fierce-looking Merritt, a Tommy gun under his arm, carries two Bren guns across a sandy beach. Below this illustration runs an excerpt from his VC citation: "When last seen he was collecting Bren and Tommy Guns and preparing a defensive position which successfully covered the withdrawal from the beach."

The courage of men like Merritt could not take the place of the heavy weapons and armoured support needed to crack the German lines. The Pourville landing had been the most effective Canadian effort of the raid. But the failure of the Canadians to silence the guns here and at Puits that overlooked the main beach at Dieppe would result in enormous casualties as the Rileys and the Essex Scottish stormed ashore.

Chapter 5
Red and White Beaches

"The defences of Dieppe town and harbour
were impregnable.
   Nobody could have taken Dieppe."
              —Lt. Col. Lord Lovat

A frontal assault on a heavily defended position, without artillery and tank support, violates every established principle of warfare. But this is what happened on the main beach of Dieppe in the early morning of August 19, 1942. And the cost in Canadian lives was horrendous.

As dawn broke at 0520 hours, half an hour after the landings on the flanks of Dieppe, the Rileys and the Essex Scottish swarmed ashore on the main beach at Dieppe. Destroyers and other naval vessels provided supporting fire. Planes from the Royal Air Force and the Royal Canadian Air Force gave protective cover to the ships, hit gun emplacements with cannon fire, and strafed the buildings on the seafront. German gunners dived for cover, and then quickly returned to their weapons to fire on the advancing Canadians. Planes laid smoke over the Eastern Headland to confuse the gunners as mortars on the landing craft lobbed smoke bombs to cover the soldiers as they scrambled over the pebbled beach.

The Germans had turned the pleasant summer resort into a fortress. The main beach of Dieppe stretched for a kilometre and a half. Festooned with barbed wire, it led up to a seawall about a metre high, topped with more barbed wire. Beyond this lay an esplanade with more tangles of wire, fronting hotels and houses that had been turned into strongpoints. Ditches in front of the seawall, dug for a drainage project, formed anti-tank barriers. To the west, Dieppe castle, a grim, grey building looked down on the length of the beach. German gunners here had a clear view of the beach and the attacking Canadians. At the eastern end of town lay a tobacco factory that had been turned into a fortress. A casino at the western end of the beach had been partially demolished and turned into a strongpoint with pillboxes built into it. Two long piers enclosed Dieppe harbour, above which loomed the Eastern Headland.

The Death Trap

Anti-tank guns, machine guns, and light artillery from caves in the cliffs zeroed in on the charging soldiers, mowing them down. An old French tank built into the harbour mole joined in the barrage. Machine-gun fire came from three directions as the Canadians jumped out of the landing craft. Mortar bombs killed their crews and set fire to them. At Dieppe, Canada's soldiers learned bitter truths about attacking enemy positions.

Some soldiers found depressions on the beach and crouched down in them. Most of them, shocked and disoriented, followed their officers to the seawall, flopped down and looked around for their friends.

Three times, the Essex Scottish on White Beach tried to cross the seawall. Three times, the soldiers were cut down. A mortar detachment fired on enemy positions until wiped out. A soldier recalled: "The beach was a deathtrap, laced by MG fire...and by mortar and shellfire."

Into the Town

The Calgary Tanks were supposed to land with the Rileys and the Essex Scottish. A navigation error delayed them by ten minutes—ten crucial minutes.

The battle for Dieppe became a stalemate. Soldiers lay behind the seawall, showered by bullets, mortar bombs, and shells, and firing blindly at the unseen enemy. Sallies into Dieppe by infantry and tanks killed and wounded some of the entrenched Germans, and the casino became the scene of hand-to-hand fighting.

Company Sergeant Major Cornelius Stapleton of the Essex Scottish breached the wire on top of the seawall and led fifteen men across the esplanade without suffering any casualties. As he put it: "I lay it ninety percent to good luck." The Canadians rampaged along Boulevard Verdun, firing from the hip at the Germans and tossing grenades into enemy-held buildings. Some of their comrades at the seawall stood up and fired incendiary grenades at enemy fortifications, setting the tobacco factory on fire. Moving towards the eastern end of the promenade, Stapleton's men saw unsuspecting German troops leaping out of a truck. They opened up on them with Sten guns, rifles, pistols, and grenades. Their ammunition expended, they headed back to the beach in their torn and tattered uniforms spotted with blood. On the way back, when a Canadian tank fired on Stapleton, he recalled his reaction: "I just took off, went across the wall, took a high dive over the wire and on to the beach."

Stapleton's sortie would have tragic consequences. He reported on it to Lt. Col. Fred Jesperson, his commanding officer, who informed the Rileys that twelve of his men had entered Dieppe. The message that reached the command ship stated: "Essex Scot across beaches and into houses." These few misleading words led General Roberts to commit the floating reserve. It comprised Les Fusiliers Mont-Royal under Lt. Col. Menard and a detachment of Royal Marine Commandos. They had been circulating offshore, awaiting the order to go into action.

The Tanks Land

The plan called for fifty-eight tanks of the 14th Canadian Army Tank Battalion (the Calgary Regiment) to land with and protect the troops as they ran up the beach and to knock out German fortifications.

Dieppe marked the first time that Churchill tanks had been sent into action in Europe. The 43-tonne monsters carried a 6-pounder (57-mm) gun, with 87 rounds of ammunition and Besa machine guns with 4,950 rounds. Manned by a crew of five, they bore names like Burns, Bob, Bolster, Cougar, and Cat. One carried the optimistic word "Confident" on its hull.

Fifty-eight tanks embarked on large landing crafts (LCTs); only twenty-nine reached Dieppe. The planners had not foreseen what would happen as the tanks roared up the beach over large pebbles. Four immediately lost their tracks while others were soon immobilized by enemy fire.

A further delay occurred when three tanks stalled because the crews had not warmed up their engines on the landing craft. Some of the tanks carried fascines, bundles of cordwood to drop into anti-tank ditches. Other had been equipped with flamethrowers. When hit, the tanks caught fire and became raging infernos, incinerating the crews. A soldier reported that as the tank named Cougar left the LCT, it was hit three or four times, but just kept moving, crushing barbed wire, which sprang back into place as soon as the tank crossed it. The tank cemented into the mole on Dieppe harbour fired on Cougar. Cougar replied, blowing the other up. Another tank, Cheetah, managed to eliminate a German pillbox. The soldiers spilling out of it were then cut down by the Essex Scottish. A third tank, pulling a staff car, drove off an LCT and went through the seawall. When last seen, "the staff car...was tearing like hell up Foch Boulevard."

Lt. Jerry Wood of the Royal Canadian Engineers made a quick reconnaissance of the beach. The LCT on which he and his men had arrived swung sideways on the shore, and was knocked out of action. Wood saw another blazing away near the casino and a sunken LCT on Red Beach. He ordered his sappers to unload the explosives and gear from the landing craft and be ready to carry them forward to blow up obstacles blocking the advance of the tanks. As they did so, he ordered the rest of his men to join him, only to discover most of them dead or wounded.

The huge landing craft made easy targets for the German artillery and snipers; machine guns killed or wounded their crews. The wheelhouse of the LCT that Wood saw near the casino had been wrecked by shellfire that killed the vessel's captain and its officers, set it on fire, and filled the hold with

Infantrymen of The Queen's Own Cameron Highlanders of Canada going ashore during the raid on Dieppe, France, August 19, 1942.

dead and wounded soldiers. But it had landed its tanks. The first went down the ramp and sank in three metres of water. The second reached the beach and headed for the seawall. The third rolled backwards, crushing two wounded soldiers before waddling out of the LCT and onto the beach where shellfire halted it by knocking off its tracks.

The Ordeal of LCT 6

No. 3 platoon of the Calgary Highlanders embarked on LCT 6 at Portsmouth under the command of Lt. Jack Reynolds. The plan called for the mortar group to set up in the tobacco factory and provide covering fire for the tanks, the Essex Scottish, and the Rileys. At 1100 hours, the men were supposed to rendezvous at a church and head back to the beach to be taken back to England.

LCT 6, captained by Lt. Thomas Andrew Cook, RN, carried a bulldozer, three tanks, and members of the Royal Army Service Corps. Tin hats were issued as the vessel ploughed across the English Channel. Men ate their rations or dozed. No one slept. At 0345 hours, night became day when the armada encountered the German convoy. Another ship nearly ran into LCT 6.

As dawn reddened the sky, the captain ordered full steam ahead and Sgt. Lyster ordered: "Mortar platoon, load rifles." To steady himself, a soldier banged the butt of his rifle on the deck. A bullet from it whizzed past Lyster's ear.

He shouted: "Save your ammunition for the beaches."

Shrapnel clanged against the sides of the landing craft as shore batteries opened up on it and shells landed in the hold. Some of the soldiers had been helping the crew peel potatoes in the galley. Reynolds ordered them out just before the galley received a direct hit, killing everyone in it. Mortar rounds exploded on the deck, and the engine room was also hit. A canister struck by shrapnel sent out fumes that overcame the helmsman. He lost control of the vessel. It yawed to port as the engine room burst into flames. Red Anderson, a member of the Calgary Highlanders, grabbed a hose and directed it at the flames, only to find himself being sprayed instead because the hose was full of holes. Another sailor took the helm, only to be shot down. The one who replaced him suffered the same fate, but the third man was luckier. Using another LCT lying broadside to the shore as a shield, he brought LCT 6 to the beach. The ramp came down, and Reynolds could see Red Beach. "Well named," he observed, gazing at the dead sprawled on the pebbles.

As shells struck the LCT, the bulldozer lurched down the ramp, its driver killed before he had driven ten metres onto the beach. The first tank followed and had its track blown off by a mine. Heavy machine-gun fire halted the second one. The third made it through the barbed wire, but Reynolds and his men could not penetrate the same barrier.

Chaos reigned on LCT 6 as the unwounded men helped

the wounded. By now, most of the vessel's crew had been killed or put out of action. The anti-aircraft guns on the ship's side stood abandoned as the vessel drifted. Reynolds ordered: "All ashore." No one from this vessel landed. Realizing that his men would stand no chance of surviving on the beach, the platoon commander ordered the mortars to be set up on the deck. They could not fire because the base plates would not hold on the sloping deck. Captain Cook took his landing craft to join the offshore fleet. Lyster and other survivors manned the anti-aircraft guns. On the way back to England, an ME 109 swooped down and sprayed LCT 6 with cannon fire. Two of the Highlanders pumped shots into its belly and saw the plane plunge into the sea.

Back in Portsmouth, after interrogation, the Calgary Highlanders received tots of rum and a hot meal. Back at their base, when a soldier reported to Sgt. Lyster: "I've lost my rifle, Sarge," he replied: "If that's all you lost, consider yourself damn lucky." A friend of the sergeant remarked: "Bert, did you ever imagine we'd be back in one piece? We're damned lucky, all of us." Lyster remarked, in words that echo those of many other survivors of the Dieppe raid: "Lucky be damned. It's a bloody miracle."

The official statement summed up the ordeal of LCT 6 by noting that "after some initial difficulties the craft reached the beach and, after fifteen minutes, the craft withdrew."

Fifteen tanks crossed the seawall or bypassed it, raced across the esplanade and headed for the town. One tank commander found every entrance into Dieppe blocked by three-metre-high concrete barriers. Sappers rushed forward to blow up these barriers only to be killed by enemy fire. The Calgary tanks moved up and down the esplanade, clearing out enemy trenches and firing on buildings before heading back to the beach to protect the soldiers there.

German propaganda photos taken after the battle show their soldiers climbing over and peering into the tanks. Obviously intrigued, they were no doubt thinking about ways of knocking them out when they next encountered them.

The Rileys: Into the Casino and the Town

The Rileys, under Lt. Col. Robert Labatt, hit White Beach under fire, moving over pebbles and finding shelter in hollowed areas. Soldiers blasted their way through barbed-wire entanglements as the Germans shot at them from the casino and a pillbox. Labatt watched as Private Hugh McCourt crawled under the barbed wire, calmly pulled a grenade from his belt and pushed it through the firing slit. The enemy position exploded. McCourt triumphantly raised his tin hat above the ruins on the end of his bayonet, signaling his comrades to join him. None did. Looking back, McCourt saw that all of them had been killed or wounded.

Captain Denis Whitaker led a section of the Rileys into the casino. Smashing through the sun veranda, hurling grenades ahead of them, they escaped from the massacre on the beach as heavy artillery installed in the northeast corner of the building thundered away at the attackers on the shore and on the ships. As the soldiers adjusted their eyes to the gloom inside the casino, one fell, fatally wounded. Private Graham then hurled grenades at the unseen enemy. Five fear-stricken Germans, hands in the air, staggered towards him.

The Rileys had to play a cat-and-mouse game in the casino as rifle fire chipped the wall behind Whitaker's head. Moving cautiously as they had been taught, the Canadians stalked the enemy along narrow corners, in alcoves, across balconies, and from room to room. Corporal McDermott crept into an auditorium, moved down the side of it behind a bar and hurled a grenade at three Germans on the stage. It was sent back. McDermott dived for cover as the blast blew the rifle from his hand. Picking up another grenade, he rushed to the stage only to find it had been abandoned. Private Oldfield, with three members of Les Fusiliers Mont-Royal, chased four Germans up a spiral staircase, trapped them in a cupboard, and eliminated them with grenades. Then he went after a nearby sniper, killing him with his bayonet.

Private Jenner reached the third floor of the casino on his own to see two of the enemy jump into a hiding place. He later said: "I shot [them] because they wouldn't come out of their hiding place when I wanted them to." Private Wilkinson ran into a corridor, weapon at the ready, to confront a German with *his* weapon at the ready. They looked at each other. The Mexican standoff ended with each dashing for cover. Four soldiers roamed the casino. When one opened a door, the others poured fire into the room or cupboard behind it. They also collected prisoners who proved to be of low quality. Their age might have made no difference if they were ensconced in strong positions. But they had no stomach for face-to-face combat, and surrendered quickly when confronted by Canadian soldiers.

Whitaker and his men reached the rear of the casino. Here a covered arcade, lined with shops on one side and columns on the other, opened onto the esplanade. Beyond this lay Boulevard Verdun along which lay buildings covered by machine guns. Four of them in the Royal Hotel opened fire on the Canadians. Private Graham took them out with his anti-tank rifle.

Searching for cover, Whitaker noticed a metre-deep trench curving to the right and leading into Dieppe. Graham jumped into it, followed by the officer and the rest of the men. Catching their breath, the Canadians realized they had landed in sewage. Whitaker led his men to a shack near the casino, only to discover that it housed a latrine. The smell drove them out of it to find shelter behind a hedge facing the seafront. From this meagre cover, they fired at the buildings opposite. Seeing two German soldiers creeping along the other side of the hedge, Sgt. Lowe cut them down as they prepared to throw grenades at his comrades. The Germans fell, their grenades exploding without harming the Canadians.

Captains E. L. McGivern and J. H. Medhurst examining a German pillbox fortification. Dieppe, France, September 3, 1944.

Mortar bombs falling nearby made the ditch look more inviting than the hedge, and the soldiers retreated to this unsavoury place. Here Lt. Dan Doherty of the FMR joined them. He had seen a burly sergeant of the Rileys with his back to the enemy, urging men on the beach to make for the casino. Seeing him unharmed, many followed his orders, with few casualties. When he reached the casino, Doherty found only dead, wounded, and captured Germans. As he put it: "I met Denis Whitaker and having nothing else to do, joined him." By now the Rileys and the FMR were fighting together to survive, ignoring the plans made for them. Whitaker and Doherty decided to attack fortified houses at the rear of the casino, but they proved too strong.

Back on the beach, a party of sappers under Sergeant George Hickson followed a platoon of Rileys around the left side of the casino. Carrying plastic explosives, they planned to use them to blow up the Dieppe telephone exchange, the post office, and the torpedo dump under the Eastern Headland. The Rileys shoved a Bangalore torpedo, a tube filled with TNT, under barbed wire in front of them. Nearby a sapper hung across it, arms and legs flailing frantically, the flaming pack of explosives on his back slowly consuming his body. The Bangalore torpedo failed to explode, so another was thrust under it. It appeared to be another dud. The sapper stood up as the torpedo exploded, removing his head. The Canadians dashed through the gap in the wire into the fire from a machine gun in a pillbox. Hickson, with two Rileys, crawled to it and put it out of action with grenades.

Realizing the futility of trying to reach his objectives, Hickson entered the casino. A soldier shouted: "They're rolling grenades down the corridors." Beckoning the soldiers into a room, Hickson told them: "If we can't get down the corridors, we'll blast our way through the walls," with a technique known as "mouse-holing." Slapping charges on the walls, Hickson turned one side of the ground floor of the casino into a mass of rubble in which lay several dead German soldiers.

Private Johnson took Hickson to a huge steel door. Behind it lay a piece of heavy artillery. Placing a charge on the door, Hickson blew it open, killing and stunning the gun crew. He destroyed the weapon with a small charge.

Eventually the casino, secured by the Rileys and the FMR, provided a passage for troops to move off the beach and reach safety. A few snipers on the third floor and the roof took potshots at them as they rushed into the ruined building. At 0712 hours, Labatt signalled to General Roberts: "Casino taken." The message confirmed the commander's belief that the attack was going well, that the Canadians were in the town, and that the time was ripe for sending in reinforcements.

Captain Tony Hill of the Rileys took a party across the esplanade to buildings on the other side of it. Breaking into a movie theatre on the Rue de Sygogne, they ran through it into Rue St. Remy and charged a German patrol with bayonets. Then they stopped and stared as a French woman came out of a house, ignored them, and entered a *boulangerie*. Emerging a few minutes later with a loaf, she returned home, still ignoring the mayhem around her. Heading along the

Rue de la Barre, the Rileys killed a sniper, and then met some Frenchmen who warned them of an advancing German patrol. Losing one man, the Canadians retreated to the movie theatre. Hill discussed blowing up the road block on the Rue de Sygogne with Major Lazier of the Royal Canadian Engineers, only to learn that the sappers had no detonators for their explosive charges. As they talked, another surreal scene unfolded. An elderly Frenchman entered the cinema, ignored the Canadians, and went about his work: he swept the floor, dusted the seats, and emptied the ashtrays.

As the Germans converged on their position, Company Sergeant Major Stewart covered the retreat of the Canadians to the casino. Hill and his men had by now spent an hour in Dieppe.

After knocking down a large part of the casino, Hickson decided to make another attempt to complete his original mission and blow up the Dieppe telephone exchange. He watched a tank lurch off the beach and over the seawall, losing a track as it reached the esplanade. It fired blindly until Whitaker had Graham fire tracers at enemy positions. The tank commander got the message and began to use his six-pounder gun to good effect on them. As enemy fire slackened, Hickson and his sappers charged across to the movie theatre without loss of men. They moved towards the Church of St. Remy and along the Rue la Martinière, only to be pinned down by sniper fire. The soldiers noted civilians wearing armbands who appeared to be pointing out the position of the Canadians to snipers. A burst of Bren gunfire dispersed them, and they retreated to the movie theatre. To reach it, they had to pass a house held by the enemy. Storming into it with Tommy guns and bayonets, they killed all inside and emerged with every one of their own number wounded. Dashing across the esplanade, all soldiers reached the safety of the casino where about 100 Rileys, FMR, signallers, and sappers held the fort.

Les Fusiliers Mont-Royal Go into Battle

By this time, the Rileys and the members of Les Fusiliers Mont-Royal had been fighting together for some time. Again, this was not part of the original plan, which called for the FMR to enter Dieppe and then cover the retreat of the Rileys and the Essex Scottish.

On board HMS *Calpe*, while Lt. Col. Menard, commander of the FMR, awaited his orders, Lt. Doherty wrote in his diary: "I was glad the steward offered me a cup of tea laced with Scotch. I had that funny feeling in my stomach and a dryness in my mouth that made the bully beef sandwich impossible to finish."

General Roberts decided to commit the FMR and the Royal Marine Commando detachment, his floating reserve, to Red Beach. Here they would reinforce the Essex Scottish, which he believed had established itself in the town. Reserve tanks would support the landing. In the fog of war, the general did not know that only the South Saskatchewans and the Camerons at Pourville had achieved any success worth supporting. And even here, large German reinforcements were on the way to drive out the invaders. Elsewhere his soldiers lay dead or wounded on the beaches of Dieppe, huddled behind the seawall or clinging to their tenuous position in the casino.

Under fire from the Western Headland and standing on the bridge of a motor launch, Menard addressed his men: "The plan is altered. We're going in right now to Red Beach."

His men would land opposite the tobacco factory, now ablaze, and attack the buildings on the seafront. If they could not cross the esplanade, they would move west and join their comrades in the casino. Menard concluded: "This is your chance to show what French Canadians can do. When you land, charge with your bayonets fixed. I will be at your head, leading you to victory." The men cheered.

Then followed one of the strangest sights of the battle at Dieppe. The small, white plywood boats carrying the FMR formed up, six abreast in four lines, and headed for Red Beach. As Sgt. Major Lucien Dumais, in one of the boats, put it: "...we were lined up as if on parade. It was a grand sight, this deployment of little white skiffs."

While crossing the Channel, Menard had wondered how many of his soldiers would survive the coming battle. He knew them well, had seen photos of their wives, families, or girlfriends. His words echo those of many soldiers going into battle for the first time: "Every man in the battalion knew a lot of us were going to get killed or hurt. But I didn't think that I was going to get killed and I don't believe a single man thought he was."

As his cockleshell armada, bright in the morning sun, neared the beach, Menard distinguished between the dull boom of heavy artillery, the chatter of machine guns, the crack of mortars, and the whine of sniper fire. They merged into a continuous roar, pressing on his eardrums, as he realized "we knew we were going into hell."

At 100 metres from the shore, the craft picked up speed as the pall of smoke that enshrouded them turned into a vortex of steel, fire, and death. Passing through the smoke screen, the boats met tracer from a hotel in front of them. Dumais ordered his Bren gunners to engage the enemy position when they landed. As enemy fire smashed into the frail craft, the sea ran red with the blood of the French-Canadian soldiers.

Dumais described the scene: "Some sank and disappeared. We stood by as they died, powerless to help...We were there to fight, not to pick up the drowning and the wounded. [The operation] was beginning to look like a disaster."

Meanwhile, Menard, his throat hot and dry, jumped ashore unscathed. He followed sappers moving to knock out a pillbox on a four-metre-high parapet, about 100 metres from the shoreline. Suddenly he fell, knocked down by a piece of shrapnel in his right shoulder; Menard described it as like being hit by a sledgehammer. Feeling no pain, he staggered to his feet, fumbling with his first-aid kit as bullets whizzed by him, wondering how to treat a wound in the right side of his body with his left hand. The second piece of shrapnel that hit the officer "seemed to shut out everything." As he advanced with his men towards the pillbox, he concluded that he was still in one piece. A third chunk of shrapnel ripped open his cheek. Crouching low, Menard saw a man ahead of him fall. A major, one of his closest friends, had taken a bullet in the stomach. Menard placed a morphine tablet on his friend's tongue: "There was nothing else I could do. He knew it and I knew it." Fueled by anger he charged forward, only to be knocked over by a bullet through his right arm. It flung him backwards onto a steel picket that damaged his spine. Pulling himself to the pillbox, Menard discovered that his men had cleared it.

By now, the FMR had their section of the beach under control, but their casualties mounted. Another piece of shrapnel hit Menard in the right knee as he struggled forward. Yet he stayed on his feet and watched his men and tanks move across the esplanade. The pain from his wounds made the officer black out, so his men carried him through fire to the beach and placed him on a boat. He came to with the sound of anti-aircraft batteries firing near his head. Looking down, Menard discovered that his men had deposited him on cases of high explosives. One bullet meant he and the boat would have disintegrated. Menard, with five wounds, realized he no longer cared a damn: "What the hell, if they haven't got me by this time, they're never going to get me."

As the ship sailed for England, a naval rating gave Menard a welcome swig of rum, and went on to serve other wounded. He returned with an anxious expression on his face. Did Menard have a stomach wound? The officer shook his head. The man relaxed and said, "That's good sir, because if you had I shouldn't have given you that rum." Menard thought this was the funniest thing he had ever heard and began to laugh. As he put it: "You see, I knew I had been through it and I felt pretty damn good..." For his bravery at Dieppe, the commander of the FMR received the Distinguished Service Order (DSO).

With the FMR on the beach, General Roberts decided to commit his last reserve—the Royal Marine Commandos and the rest of the tanks—to support the Rileys. The British troop headed towards Dieppe in boats manned by Free French Chasseurs as gunboats provided covering fire. The commander of the Chasseurs observed: "I realized that this attack was to be a sea parallel to the Charge of the Light Brigade." As they passed out of the smoke screen into the brilliant morning sunshine, shells from the headlands and machine-gun fire from the houses on the promenade took a toll on the crew of the assault boats and the Commandos. Lt. Col. Phillips, commander of the Royal Marines, realizing the impossibility of landing on White Beach, stood up in the bow of a landing craft. Donning a pair of white gloves to ensure that he would be seen by his men, and with his back to the enemy, the officer shouted: "For God's sake go back..." as a stream of tracer bullets cut him down. Five of the assault craft turned around while two others hit the beach and dropped their ramps. Only a handful of marines survived the hail of bullets directed at them, rushing up the beach to find shelter behind a disabled tank.

As LCT 8 approached the beach, Lt. Col. John Andrews, commander of the Calgary Tanks, sat waiting impatiently to land. A shell cut the chains of the ramp, sending it crashing into the water. Andrews ordered his tank down the ramp. It sank. The crew bailed out. Andrews's body was later seen floating near the beach; he had been killed by a sniper.

The captain, officers, and all but one of the crew of LCT 8 had been killed, along with some senior Canadian soldiers on board. The vessel's engineer, the sole survivor, had been blown into the water through a hole in the side of the vessel. As the landing craft drifted helplessly under enemy shelling, its decks covered with dead and wounded, a Canadian staff officer rushed below and restarted the engines. A marine grabbed the helm and took the vessel away from the shore and through the shell-pocked sea. Suddenly the engineer, soaking wet, leapt aboard the LCT from an assault craft. He was determined to take his ship back to England. Under the protection of a smokescreen, LCT 8, taken in tow, reached port safely.

Sergeant Dubuc Goes to Town

Sergeant Pierre Dubuc came ashore just west of the casino, ran 100 metres, and threw himself into the dubious safety of a hollow on the beach as machine-gun bullets streamed overhead. Like other members of the FMR, he decided he would not stay in front of two pillboxes whose inhabitants wanted to kill him. Private Daudelin joined the sergeant, dragging a smoke generator. Dubuc told him to start it up. Under its choking fumes, the two Canadians advanced to the pillboxes and dropped grenades into them. Noticing an abandoned tank, they edged towards it, crept inside, and fired its remaining ammunition against enemy guns on the Western Headland, under which eleven of their comrades crouched.

Daudelin decided his chances of survival would be better if he left Dubuc, who signalled to the soldiers huddled under the Western Headland to join him. They dashed into Dieppe under machine-gun fire. Capturing the crew of one of them, they killed them, since it was not possible to hold prisoners. Charging along streets, the Canadians reached the inner harbour of Dieppe: Bassin Duquesne and Bassin du Canada. (From the latter, settlers and their goods had once embarked for New France.) Dubuc's men attacked two barges in the harbour, expending their ammunition. Then they looked for cover, expecting the Royal Marine Commandos to arrive and support them. Instead a German patrol attacked from three sides and the little band surrendered.

Taken to a courtyard, the FMR were ordered in English to undress. Dubuc informed their captors in French that, as French Canadians, they could not obey an order given in English. One of the Germans growled "undress" in French, and the soldiers complied. Departing with their clothes and weapons, the enemy left their captives under the guard of a youngster. Dubuc, licking his lips, asked him if he spoke English. The boy nodded. "Would it be possible," the sergeant asked, "to get a drink of water on this hot day?" When the German looked around for a tap, the Canadians jumped on him and killed him. Then they took off for the beach in their underwear.

The scene that followed resembled a French farce.

Dubuc ran past Frenchmen and giggling girls amused by the sight of a man in his skivvies. Encountering a German patrol, the sergeant ran around it as its members broke into uproarious laughter. Canadians in the casino and Germans in the seafront buildings ceased firing at each other as they watched the half-naked figure hurtle along the esplanade. Dubuc jumped over the seawall and collapsed, panting and dripping with sweat. The battle-weary face of a sergeant in the Rileys loomed over the exhausted man, demanding: "Who are you?"

"Sergeant Pierre Dubuc, Fusiliers Mont-Royal," gasped the exhausted runner.

The Riley grunted: "Then where the hell have you been out of uniform?"

Sergeant Major Dumais's Story

Sergeant Major Dumais had been optimistic when he left England. He had been told that the enemy was not particularly strong at Dieppe, nor its defences extensive. He had soon been disabused of these ideas during the landing and subsequent events as he led his FMR comrades into battle.

Now at 1100 hours, as the *Vanquish* order to withdraw reached him, he rushed for one of the last rescue boats to leave Dieppe. Grabbing a rope hanging from its side, he hung on desperately. His equipment and steel helmet pulled him down and he sank like a stone. This would be the way his life ended, the soldier mused, as the waters of Dieppe closed over him.

But Dumais did not drown.

He lived to continue his remarkable military career, ending the war as a captain with the Military Medal and the Military Cross for his exploits at Dieppe and elsewhere. Dumais's book, *The Man Who Went Back,* provides a graphic account of how many Canadians soldiers fared on that dire summer day in 1942.

Dumais joined Les Fusiliers Mont-Royal in 1934 at the age of twenty-nine, so was much older than most of his comrades. He describes himself as being small in stature, "touchy, quarrelsome, and determined to excel in all I do." In the pre-war years, Dumais spent only fifteen days a year training for combat. Called to active service, he took a commando course and learned to use his own initiative.

As a young man, Dumais dreamed of travelling to France. His arrival there proved very different from anything he could have imagined. He writes of his landing craft gliding over a calm sea under a clear sky "sprinkled with stars that shone like jewels on blue velvet." Looking at his men sleeping like children, he wondered how many would survive the coming battle. Dawn came, a brilliant pink with a slight haze hovering over the surface of the sea, promising a fine summer's day.

The men awoke, and Dumais ordered them to shave in sea water: "In the best tradition, we could not die without a shave and shiny boots." Scrounging a rag from a sailor, Dumais polished his boots with it and then passed it around to the others. The soldiers had little food, so Dumais found emergency rations and shared them "to ensure no one would die hungry."

In his book, Dumais summarizes his feelings as the boats neared the beach: "It would be the first time the name of our regiment was mentioned in a battle, and we had to uphold the tradition that the veterans of the last war had handed down to us."

After he explained the plan of attack to his men, they played cards: "I think that if they had to wait at the gates of hell, they would sit down and start shuffling."

The half-decked plywood boats carried twenty soldiers, and offered no protection to them as they came within sight of the enemy coast and under fire. Through binoculars, Dumais scanned the beach, seeing an LCT burning near the casino, troops on the beach and behind the seawall firing at enemy positions, and tanks pouring shots into the town.

To Dumais "it seemed crazy to go in."

But in went the French Canadian soldiers at 0700 hours.

Mortar bombs landed near Dumais's boat, shrapnel from them piercing its thin side and wounding two men. Everyone on board tried to make himself as small as possible. Dumais saw a friend in another boat jerk upright and tumble into the water. As mortar bombs landed nearby and machine-gun fire holed the fragile craft, Dumais reflected: "I had a very curious feeling of self-pity. I began to think the enemy was definitely unreasonable to be doing this to me, it was very dangerous and he might kill me."

Dumais directed two Bren gunners to cover the men as they leapt ashore. As the boat backed away and men swam through a blood-red sea to reach it, a sniper killed the captain. Fusiliers in other boats jumped into shoulder-deep water to avoid machine-gun bullets shredding the sides of their small craft. The one carrying Dumais's mortar and bombs moved out to sea; he and his men would have to fight as infantrymen.

Dumais compared being on the beach to standing "in the middle of a very busy intersection with traffic from four directions, and it made me dizzy." Getting his bearings, half-crouching, he headed for the casino, dropping down once to convince enemy snipers he had been hit. His platoon commander Lt. Pierre Loranger fell, wounded in both legs. Dumais took over from him, picking up his maps and Sten gun, and moving behind a tank while trying to determine where the enemy fire originated. Another soldier followed him, nestling down behind one of the tank's tracks. It suddenly backed up, crushing him. A soldier stood up in front of the machine as its Besa machine gun opened fire, removing his head. Looking around, Dumais saw numerous dead and wounded men, some unmoving, some groaning, some screaming in agony, their shattered bodies pouring out dark red blood onto the pebbles.

The sergeant major had very few men with him.

He watched three members of his platoon dash across the esplanade under machine-gun fire. Privates Ulric and Simard made it to cover, but Private Marechal fell, hit in the stomach. The firing stopped as the wounded man writhed in agony, holding in his guts with his clasped hands. Simard jumped from cover, dashed across to Marechal, and dragged him to safety as machine-gun bullets spattered around him.

Moving up the west side of the casino, Dumais encountered a German and killed him; it was the first time he had ever done this. Dumais recognized his reaction to the killing as being neither one of pity or remorse but of "purely professional indifference." He had reacted faster than the enemy soldier; he was dead and Dumais was alive.

Entering the casino, choking on dust in the dim light, Dumais found nothing but broken glass, ripped wood, and shattered plaster with dead and wounded soldiers on the floor. Seeing a machine gunner firing on the beach, he aimed his Sten at him. It jammed, a common failing of this weapon. Picking up a discarded rifle, Dumais went in search of the enemy. A sudden explosion knocked him down. Sergeant Hickson had blown open the casement built into the side of the casino.

Returning under fire to the beach, Dumais found a few fit, unwounded soldiers and ordered them to follow him. Another soldier, crouching down and crying, was paralyzed by an uncontrollable fear. The sergeant major took his band into town after collecting more stray soldiers. His luck held out: "By rights I should have been dead hours ago: I must be bullet proof."

Arranging covering fire from the windows of the casino, Dumais ordered seven men to follow him across the esplanade, over a three-metre-high barrier, past an abandoned German anti-tank gun towards St. Remy church. Then they retreated. Germans cut them down as Dumais covered them with a Bren gun.

Back on the beach, having failed to escape, the sergeant major found shelter with scores of wounded men huddled near a burning LCT. After trying to organize a defence perimeter, Dumais shared his water with the wounded, dashing out under fire to recover water bottles from those who had no further use for them. By now, he had realized: "Nothing was working out as planned. I realized that things were not very bright."

By 1300 hours, things had quieted down. Tanks lay abandoned on the beach strewn with dead, dying, and wounded Canadians. Landing craft bobbed up and down on the incoming tide, some on fire, others crowded with mounds of casualties. Ammunition on the burning vessels exploded from time to time, shattering the silence descending on this desolate killing ground. Any activity, any movement, even by men writhing in agony, brought a hail of fire. In time, it, too, tailed off.

The seven-metre tide advanced on wounded men too weak to move. Dumais decided it was time to surrender to save their lives. He saw no point in mounting a last stand that no one would hear about as he looked at his companions, their faces streaked with dirt and blood, their uniforms torn, grimy, and soaked with sea water.

As he stood awaiting his captors, Dumais jammed his rifle upside down into the pebbles on the beach as a sign of surrender: "It seemed to symbolize the fact that my military career was over." It wasn't.

But that's another story.

Chapter 6
Withdrawal

*"Destroy what can be destroyed...it is up to
us now...to wipe out as many of the enemy...
in any way possible...Every available
weapon must now contribute to the
complete destruction of the enemy."*
—Field Marshal Gerd von Runstedt,
German Commander-in-Chief (West)

The sense of utter futility that overwhelmed Sgt. Major
Dumais as he surrendered to save the lives of his comrades
was shared by many of the survivors of the battle. Sergeant Ed
Bennett of the Essex Scottish, his whole face burned off, told
his men: "Remember, boys, if it comes, give only your name,
rank, and number."

The evacuation of the attacking forces began as the signal "Vanquish 1100" reached their commanders. By this time, the German Air Force had arrived in strength over the fleet and the beaches. Ross Munro reported: "Several landing craft blew up, hit by bombs and cannon shells. There was nothing left. They just disintegrated."

Otto Hasibeder, a German radio operator, became bewildered at what was happening as the landing craft came in, under fire, to take the troops off the beach:

> *Then; after two, three hours...it really dawned*
> *on me that this was an impossible thing.*
> *More and more boats were sunk...some*
> *[soldiers] tried to escape, to get to the boats*
> *and were shot down. Bombs were dropped*
> *and artillery was firing. I couldn't even think*
> *clearly any more. I took messages and looked*
> *at the thing. I said, "How long can this go on?"*

If the Dieppe landings had been a horrendous experience for Canadian soldiers, their withdrawal proved even more terrible. As the small boats of the Royal Navy headed for the main beach, planes laid smoke to cover the retreat, making it difficult for those of HMS *Calpe*, the command ship, to determine what was happening. Snipers continued to pick off officers and NCOs. Lt. Col. Fred Jesperson, commander of the

Essex Scottish, admitted: "We were all afraid...The experience was harrowing and how I was missed God only knows." Some of his men had entered the town, but most still remained on the beach, each trying to make himself as small a target as possible. The scene remained forever rooted in Jesperson's mind. The soldiers could not advance over the fire-swept seawall and esplanade. Nor could they retreat to the shoreline to await the rescue boats without fear of instant death. Those lucky enough to reach the edge of the water found protection in and around the beached landing craft.

And yet the Canadians kept on fighting.

Jesperson saw Major Willis, wounded in the chest, arms, and head, directing the fire of his company. Lt. Green, his foot shot off by shrapnel from a mortar bomb, had it bound up and then continued to lead his platoon until a second mortar bomb finished him.

Compassion on the Beach

From time to time, downed German pilots drifted ashore in their rubber dinghies. Trembling with fear, they approached the Canadians. They had been told they would be shot if they fell into enemy hands. One crawled to the seawall on Red Beach, his face showing his fears. Jesperson felt only compassion for this young, white-faced, fearful man. A sergeant tied the airman's hands behind his back, lit a cigarette, and put it in his mouth. Jesperson moved around, giving morphine to the wounded, encouraging his men, glancing anxiously to sea. An anguished soldier cried out: "For God's sake, someone surrender." An officer shouted: "No one surrenders, you hear me?"

Lt. Col. Labatt, commander of the Rileys, urged his men to reach the casino, pass through it, and attack enemy positions on the seafront. Heavy fire sweeping the esplanade made this increasingly impossible. Wounded men pulled themselves, slowly and painfully, to the seaward side of landing craft on the shoreline. The craft were crowded with dead, dying, and wounded. Doctors, medics, and fellow soldiers moved among the wounded, doing what they could for them. Padre John Foote, chaplain of the Rileys, had "stowed away" on one of the attack boats to be with his men. On White Beach he tended to the wounded at the Regimental Aid Post (RAP). Time and again, he left its shelter to give morphine, offer comfort to the dying, and carry badly wounded men to the RAP. As the dead bobbed up and down on the incoming tide, Foote pulled soldiers in danger of dying out of the water. When the rescue boats arrived, the padre took a man on his back and waded to one of them as soldiers frantically tried to board it. He persuaded some of them to put the wounded man on the vessel. Then he returned to the beach and carried another man to it. He continued rescuing men for an hour, carrying them on his back as the Germans kept up relentless fire on the beach and the boats. Shouting, "Every man carry a man," he saved at least thirty lives.

Two soldiers tried to pull Foote aboard the last boat to leave. He freed himself from their helpful hands and returned to the beach. As he put it: "It seemed to me the men ashore in all likelihood will need me far more in the months of captivity ahead than any of those going home." For his selfless dedication to his comrades, John Foote received the Victoria Cross, the only member of the Royal Canadian Army Chaplain Corps to be so honoured.

About 200 of Les Fusiliers Mont-Royal huddled under the protection of an overhanging cliff below the Western Headland. Some had landed in a craft commanded by Lieutenant R. F. McCrae, senior Canadian naval officer at Dieppe. Riddled by machine guns, with huge holes in its sides, the vessel had become an instant wreck on landing, its hold filled with dead and wounded soldiers. McCrae and his crew moved among them, doing what they could for the living, administering morphine, binding up wounds, and keeping up morale. The Germans looked down upon them, recognized that this stranded aid post did not represent a threat to them, and left those on board to continue their work of mercy.

"Every Man for Himself!"

Each unit became responsible for its own withdrawal as soldiers swarmed down the beach to the rescue ships. Discipline broke, and it became every man for himself—with fatal results. Soldiers clambered aboard boats, overwhelming them, bogging them down, making it difficult for the captains to reverse and clear the beach.

As the first boats reached the shore, hundreds of soldiers—Essex Scottish, Rileys, Fusiliers, sappers and others—rose from shelter in hollows, from behind the seawall and the protection of stalled tanks, and frantically made for them. The Germans held their fire until the men bunched up at the ramps of the rescue vessels. Then they poured fire into their backs. Lt. Wood of the Royal Canadian Engineers, tending wounded near a stranded LCT observed: "We ran out of stretchers, bodies had to be piled high to make room for the living." He shouted at soldiers rushing the boats to help him get the wounded on board: "I should have saved my breath." A badly wounded man made for the water, crawling on his hands and knees, reaching the shore only to be knocked down by the advancing waves. Wood and two others rushed out to pull him, and another soldier floating nearby, to safety.

The retreat from the casino took place in a disciplined manner.

German prisoners carried wounded Canadians out of the casino on stretchers and doors. Men ran along the sun veranda, through the wire, and onto the beach, protected by a rearguard of four officers: Denis Whitaker, Dan Doherty, Tony Hill, and Harold Lazier. A smokescreen enshrouded the Rileys as they reached the boats. The smoke suddenly lifted and all hell broke loose as the overcrowded vessels pushed away

German troops examining a Churchill tank of the Calgary Regiment abandoned during the raid on Dieppe, August 19, 1942.

from shore. A shell burst in one of them with ghastly results as the sea filled with bobbing heads and the desperate waving arms of drowning men.

Stripping off his uniform, Labatt swam towards a tank landing craft. At 200 yards short of it, he saw the boat take two direct hits and sink. The officer said aloud: "How bloody stupid," and swam back to the beach. Utterly tired and completely chilled, he took shoes, socks, and a duffle coat off a dead man. Looking around, the commander of the Rileys realized the futility of continuing the fight. The wounded could not hold their weapons and many of the unwounded, in the rush for boats, had thrown theirs away.

To protect the men sheltering near an LCT, a tank kept firing. An officer rushed out, waving a white flag. Since the tank was still in operation, surrender was not acceptable to either side. The officer went down, his body riddled by the bullets of the enemy and of his own men.

Sgt. Hickson left the casino, avoiding enemy fire directed at soldiers bunched up near the boats. He reached one, jumped on board, and was followed by others. Their weight jammed the ramp. The captain took the boat off the beach as Hickson ordered the men to bale it out with their tin hats. To encourage them, he tried to start a singsong, but found himself doing a solo and gave up.

Sgt. Major Stewart boarded an assault boat. Overloaded, it sank in two minutes. He took to the water, swimming for two-and-a-half hours before being rescued. Major MacRae of the Essex Scottish found an abandoned lifeboat. Filling it with wounded soldiers with the help of others, he launched it into the water. After pushing the boat ahead of him for three kilometres, MacRae reached a gunboat just as he slipped into unconsciousness.

The tanks that had reached the esplanade turned, rattled over the seawall, and dispersed along the beach to provide protective fire for the soldiers trying to reach the rescue boats. Slowly but surely, each Churchill tank, immobilized by German guns, ran out of ammunition. At 1105 hours, Major Alan Glenn, the commander of the Calgary

Tanks, ordered his men to bail out and make for the shelter of the landing craft. Only one of them, Private Volk, a gunner, escaped capture by swimming from the beach and being rescued.

Three kilometres offshore, as an assault boat sank, an LCT took eighty men off it. They included Dollard Menard and Private Leo Belair, who was looking after his colonel. Water poured in and the craft began to sink. Everything movable, including a group of German prisoners, went overboard.

At 1100 hours, General Roberts ordered HMS *Calpe* to run for the shore under a smokescreen in a last, desperate effort to pick up men from the beach, although he could see no movement there. The destroyer swung around, rescued a few swimmers, and headed for England, her decks crowded with wounded and exhausted men. A Focke Wulf 190 dropped a bomb on the ship, killing two men near Quentin Reynolds and knocking out one of his gold teeth inlays, but otherwise leaving him unharmed.

At 1340 hours, General Roberts sent a message by pigeon:

> *Very heavy casualties in men and ships.*
> *Did everything possible to get men off but*
> *in order to get any home had to come to sad*
> *decision to abandon remainder.*

The bird reached its loft at 1655 hours, long after the battle at Dieppe had ended.

About 500 men were lifted from the beaches at Dieppe. Reynolds, on HMS *Calpe*, wrote of its decks and wardroom packed with silent men, their faces marked by fear, pain, and fatigue, their eyes staring, and walking jerkily like punch-drunk fighters.

On the beach, the firing slowly faltered, then ended, save for a few random shots, as the last rescue ships withdrew and the air battle moved into the skies above the Channel. In Dieppe castle, a German officer phoned General Haase: "The British Navy has gone. Remnants of the landing force are still holding out. Request permission to clear up the battlefield."

As soldiers of Germany's 571st Infantry Division approached the beaches, white flags rose from the scattered groups of Canadian soldiers. A strange exchange of courtesies took place. Canadian officers sent German airmen who had drifted ashore to the advancing soldiers. The German infantry, in return, allowed Canadians to rescue helpless men lying near the shoreline in danger of drowning.

Major Gordon Rolfe placed his signal and code books in a neat pile on the pebbles, set fire to them, and tossed a grenade at his staff car to deny it to the enemy. He could not persuade Brigadier William Southam to part with his copy of the Operation Jubilee plan. Instead, this officer shouted: "We must not surrender. There's the enemy. Why doesn't someone shoot?"

Southam had with him copy number 37 of the plan for the operation which specified how prisoners would be bound up when captured. The officer tried to hide it in the pebbles on the beach. A sharp-eyed German officer saw what Southam was doing and retrieved the document. Its contents had dire consequences for Canadians captured at Dieppe and for other invaders of Hitler's Europe.

When the Germans learned about the way that prisoners had been tied up and that some of them had been killed, they ordered that officers and men captured at Dieppe be shackled. On October 19, 1942, Hitler issued a special order, directing that "all enemies on so-called Commando missions in Europe and Asia...are to be slaughtered to the last man."

In later years, Paul Dumaine of the FMR recalled his experiences at Dieppe. An hour after landing, wounded in the head, he collapsed on the beach: "I stayed a long time there just doing nothing. I couldn't walk. It was like I was paralyzed. I was bleeding and I wanted to get up...But I couldn't. My legs were paralyzed from the shock of my injury. I had to drag myself by my elbows to the ocean. I washed my head with water."

This sense of being paralyzed, from wounds or shock, was a common battle phenomenon and affected many Canadians soldiers during this first encounter with an enemy trying to kill them.

Sheltering behind a tank, Dumaine saw a downed German pilot float towards the beach in his dinghy:

Withdrawal

*He came to me with his arms up yelling
"Kamerad! Kamerad!" [Surrender!] He
sat beside me...took some photos from
his pocket and...showed me his wife and
children. He wanted to soften my heart so
that we would not kill him...I didn't pay
him any attention; I couldn't speak German.
He stayed there until the end of the battle.*

Dumaine added: "The battle was poorly organized. We lost everything we had to lose. I was injured and taken prisoner."

Dumaine's words echo the thoughts of many of the Canadian soldiers, wounded and unwounded, as they lay under enemy fire on the beach, unable to move, unable to do anything other than keep their heads down and pray that a bullet or piece of shrapnel did not have their name on it. As the battle ended, they also began to contemplate their bleak future as prisoners-of-war. In this, as in the fighting, some were luckier than others.

Howard Large's war ended before the withdrawal began. As the Essex Scottish stormed the seawall, he saw a friend blown up by a Bangalore torpedo. With twenty of his comrades, Large dashed across the esplanade; only seven men reached a house on the other side of it. Unaware of the presence of the Canadians, a German patrol entered the house: "The seven of us fired our guns down the hallway. They had come in and they were laughing...And then there was no more laughing, not even a moan. We got the whole patrol."

Wounded in the leg, Large put a tourniquet on to stem the bleeding and stumbled into the basement of the house. A German patrol came down the stairs and fired at him even as he shouted that he was wounded. "When I got upstairs... the dead bodies of the other fellows were there. One soldier put a rifle right to my head. Another pushed it away, and said, in English: 'This is my prisoner.'" The Germans laid Large out with other wounded soldiers on the lawn in front of the house, he recounted, and then "a lady came out...with a tray of beer and offered it to us. They handed me one before they took one for themselves. The best beer I ever had, right until this day."

Another captured soldier reported: "The Germans took our rifles...They were quite easygoing. Everyone felt relief." German photos from the time show their medics attending wounded Canadian soldiers, and officers standing at ease with other captives.

On August 19, the German War Diary in the headquarters of the Commander-in-Chief West noted: "1740 hours. No armed Englishmen remains on the Continent."

On HMS *Calpe*, as it sped for England, Quentin Reynolds met General Roberts: "'It was tougher than you figured, wasn't it?' I asked. He drew a deep breath. 'Yes,' he said slowly. 'It was tougher than we figured.'"

Chapter 7
The Air Battle

*"...it was the greatest air show since the
Battle of Britain in the fall of 1940, and
the RAF and the RCAF had overwhelming
superiority."*

—Ross Munro

Lucien Dumais recalled the first attack on the convoy on its
way to France when a Focke Wulf appeared from nowhere
"making straight for us." The ships opened fire on the plane,
joined by soldiers with rifles, Stens, and Bren guns. The
plane turned away in a half-roll, black smoke trailing from
its engine: "We could see the pilot struggling to get out of his
cockpit, but it was too late." Everyone cheered as the flame-
and smoke-enshrouded plane plunged into the sea.

Some of the last casualties of the Dieppe raid originated with a chance act, not a planned attack. Pursued by fighters, a German Ju88 jettisoned a bomb. It hit the destroyer HMS *Berkeley* amidships, destroying the bridge and wardroom, flooding the boiler and engine rooms, and breaking the warship's back. The bomb killed the *Berkeley*'s captain and a Royal Air Force wing commander observing the air battle, and hurled Lt. Col. Hillsinger of the United States Army Air Force onto the foredeck. The American had recently bought a pair of hand-made shoes in London. Now one of them floated nearby, with his right foot inside it. Hillsinger took off the other shoe and flung it into the water, shouting, "Take the goddam pair."

A gunboat came alongside the destroyer to take off wounded and to rescue the crew. A sailor carried Hillsinger aboard. Sitting on the deck, the airman refused anything but the necessary medical treatment for his wound. He stayed in the open, explaining, "I'm meant to be observing the air battle."

The *Berkeley* could not be saved so she was torpedoed and sunk by HMS *Albrighton*. She was the largest of the more than a quarter of the ships that the Royal Navy lost in Operation Jubilee.

One objective of the Dieppe raid was to lure the Luftwaffe, the German air force, into battle and draw some of their planes away from Russia. Whether Operation Jubilee drew any aircraft

The Air Battle

Douglas Boston aircraft of the Royal Air Force taking part in Operation Jubilee, the raid on Dieppe, August 19, 1942.

from the eastern front is dubious, but the plan to bring the Luftwaffe to battle succeeded—at great cost to the Allies: The RAF and RCAF lost 106 aircraft, the largest toll of any single day since the war had begun. They suffered 153 casualties in 2,000 sorties, including eight pilots killed and one taken as a prisoner-of-war. The newspaper headlines screamed that 200 German planes had been destroyed. Air Vice-Marshal Leigh Mallory, head of Fighter Command, claimed that 91 German aircraft had been "officially destroyed and about twice that number have probably been destroyed and damaged." In fact, the Germans lost 48 bombers and fighters and had 24 damaged.

Quentin Reynolds, on HMS *Calpe,* told about the arrival of the German bombers over the invasion fleet: "I watched two Dorniers die, falling like orange fire into the sea. A third met a shell squarely in midair and simply came apart, a mass of scattering debris."

Every ship in the fleet kept moving to avoid becoming a stationary target, while their guns threw up tracer and flak. In the confusion, they shot down six Spitfires.

The Essex Scottish manned some of the anti-aircraft guns on the landing fleet. Their commander, Lt. Col. Guy Gostling, brother of Alfred who was killed leading the Camerons on White Beach, watched his men fire on two Boston medium bombers that were escorted by Spitfires. The naval gunners on his tank landing craft had opened up on them, and the Canadians had followed suit. Gostling dashed up to the bridge and asked the first officer he met why the guns were firing on their own planes. He received a "non-committal reply" so asked a gunner what he was firing at: "A Focke Wulfe torpedo bomber," came the reply. By then the planes were out of range. Gostling added: "We were recompensed for our mistakes by having the escort of fighters spray us liberally with machine-gun fire."

The RAF and RCAF did what they could to support the

attacking troops. The RAF deployed forty-two Spitfire squadrons, the RCAF six. The Royal New Zealand Air Force also took part in the air battle. The Germans sent up 200 fighters to protect bombers attacking ships and to strafe the troops on the ground. The war in the air was as confused and chaotic as that on the ground.

At 0512 hours, eight minutes before the soldiers landed, the first Allied naval salvo crashed on the enemy positions, and planes laid down smoke over the East Headland and strafed the seafront.

Flight Lieutenant John Godfrey of RCAF 412 Squadron arrived on the scene at 0600 hours: "Over Dieppe it had been impossible to keep the squadron together and everybody split into twos: The sky was filled with a swirling mass of Spitfires and FW 190s milling around..."

Godfrey saw a shot-down pilot step off his sinking plane onto a navy ship without getting his feet wet. Godfrey's own plane was hit by flak. He nursed it back to RAF Tangmere in Sussex and examined the damage. A piece of shrapnel had penetrated the metal seat of the plane, and had lodged in the parachute pack on which Godfrey sat. A few millimetres of silk had saved the Canadian pilot from serious injury.

British and Canadian Spitfires engaged German bombers and their accompanying fighters. They also protected Hurricanes attacking enemy ground positions with cannon fire.

The United States Army Air Corps sent B17s (Flying

Fortresses) to bomb the German airfield at Abbeville, a few kilometres from Dieppe.

The Germans held their reserves, including a panzer unit, behind the beaches, ready to go into action if the enemy broke through the first defences. The Dieppe raid was based on withdrawing the troops before this happened. The Canadian Army Cooperation Squadron flew forty-two missions to give warnings of when German reinforcements were moving towards Dieppe.

Bostons, some from RCAF 418 Squadron, attempted to bomb the Berneval and Varengeville batteries overlooking the main beach and the sea approaches to it; they missed their targets. One Boston with engine trouble was shot down, but its crew survived. Five squadrons of cannon-firing fighters sprayed the esplanade and other parts of Dieppe but did little damage. The lucky shot that blew up the ammunition dump at Varengeville represented the only significant achievement of the air forces in the battle at Dieppe. The smoke they laid down doubtless saved some lives, but it kept blowing away at crucial times, exposing the attackers to enemy fire. The air battle featured yet one more example of poor communication that hampered the operation. A request to bomb German batteries, sent at 1144 hours was not received until 1330 hours—after the battle had ended.

One of the reasons given for the failure of Operation Jubilee was the absence of large warships and their powerful guns and of heavy bombers that would have destroyed German gun positions. In retrospect, this decision saved numerous French lives. The art of firing upon or dropping bombs on enemy targets was by no means precise at this stage of the war. RAF Air Vice-Marshal Harris, convinced that he could end the war by flattening German cities and destroying the will of their residents to fight—a belief that proved fallacious—refused to release any of his heavy bombers to Operation Jubilee. This proved to be an example of doing the right thing for the wrong reason. Dieppe might have suffered the same fate as Caen did after D-Day. Before the Allied landings in Normandy on June 6, 1944, hundreds of bombers plastered roads, railway junctions, enemy emplacements, and other strategic locations. About 20,000 French men, women, and children died during these attacks.

Chapter 8
Aftermath

"Have just returned from a day trip to France. Stop. It was very hot and I did not enjoy myself. Stop."
—Telegram sent by a Dieppe survivor

The Dieppe raid has been the subject of thirty books in English and French, one in German, half-a-dozen TV documentaries or docudramas, an epic poem, and at least three short ones. On May 6, 1946, the name of Leger Corner, New Brunswick, now a suburb of Moncton, was changed to Dieppe to commemorate the battle. In his book about the battle, Greenhous writes: "Dieppe, Dieppe. In Canadian ears the word resounds with all the ritual solemnity of a funeral bell."

A German interrogating Major Brian McCool, Principal

Disembarkation of wounded troops (in England) during Operation Jubilee, the raid on Dieppe, August 19, 1942.

Military Landing Officer on the main beach, asked him: "Look, McCool, it was too big for a raid and too small for an invasion. What was it?" McCool replied: "If you can tell me the answer I would be most grateful."

Denis Whitaker, who later commanded the Rileys and ended his army career as a brigadier, looking back at the battle in which he fought so bravely, concluded: "My hardest lesson...after all my years of careful and often painful research was in not finding pat answers to everything. Gaps will always remain in the 'how' and 'why.'"

In his poem "Dieppe," George Whalley catches the fierce joy of men going into battle: "Ebbed now the cold fear that turns the will to water."

The words of a survivor of Blue Beach ring with fury about what happened there: "Every man knew his job and was eager to get a crack at the enemy. We wanted to give a damn good show, to the world, to Canada and the Germans... Everything seemed to go wrong...We felt robbed of the chance to fight and show what we could do."

Able Seaman Albert Smith reflected on how he was "so proud of the way the Camerons went to their deaths. So sad that they seem to have been wasted."

In short, there was nothing wrong with the calibre of the Canadian troops who fought at Dieppe. The fault for the failure of Operation Jubilee lies in the higher ranks of the military and the politics of command.

Lord Lovat, whose Commandos had shown what could be achieved with a quick raid on a defined target, commented: "Looking back, one thing is certain—never postpone an operation and then remount it after an appreciable delay." The morale of the Canadian troops who had embarked for Operation Rutter in early July was high. When that was cancelled, their mood became subdued and apprehensive because they believed the Germans knew they were coming. Ross Munro, in a landing craft with eighty soldiers, reported: "Even before we put to sea some had an ominous feeling about what was ahead of them at the other side."

Did the Germans know the Canadians were coming?

A German prisoner interrogated by Denis Whitaker claimed they did. The official explanation has always been that they did not. The Germans were acutely aware, after several raids on their coastal areas, that another was possible. They placed their soldiers on alert in mid-August because conditions were right for another raid.

Lovat claimed that the Canadians soldiers were not really aware of the magnitude of their task, and that high courage and ordinary infantry training "are no answer to machine-gun fire and impregnable fortifications, set in cliffs." He added that planning by Combined Operations and coordination between army, navy, and air force had not "at that time reached the high standard that was subsequently achieved."

The disaster at Dieppe has been presented as a "dress rehearsal" for D-Day, the invasion of France on June 6, 1944. In his history of the Second World War, Winston Churchill wrote that the grim casualties "must not class it as a failure. It was a costly but not unfruitful reconnaissance-in-force...a vital part of our agreed offensive policy." Operation Jubilee paid off for the British Prime Minister. On July 25, after Operation Rutter had been cancelled, he received a phone call from Stalin, asking him what was being done to distract the Germans by raids on occupied territory. Churchill told the Russian dictator that action was in hand and that he had given highest priority to Operation Jubilee. In response to others pressing for action, after what happened on August 19, he could indicate the need for improvements in equipment, troops, and other matters before any other attempts were planned to land in France or elsewhere on the continent.

One apologist made some strange claims by stating that each life lost at Dieppe saved ten on D-Day. Richard Hough in *The Longest Battle* states: "The lessons learned were of critical importance in the planning and execution of the invasion almost two years later saving many more lives than were lost in the operations." But this conclusion has been questioned in recent years. Greenhous writes: "Few, if any, lessons were learned that could not have been learned just as effectively, and far more cheaply by intelligent analysis of possibilities and technology and the application of common sense to properly thought-out training."

The Oxford Companion to World War II ends its entry on "Dieppe raid" as follows: "Jubilee is not now seen by all historians as being an essential prerequisite to any full-scale invasion of France. Some regard it as an unjustifiable gamble which, without adequate air and sea support, had no chance of success."

Operation Jubilee presents an example of how history is interpreted and reinterpreted over the years. It also supports the saying: "Victory has a hundred fathers, but defeat is an orphan."

One factor, beyond the personalities involved, contributed greatly to what happened on the beaches of Dieppe on August 19: institutional incompetence. Bad planning, bad management, bad decisions.

Who Was Responsible?

General Andrew McNaughton, commander of the British Army, always insisted that the responsibility for making Operation Jubilee a largely Canadian operation was his and no one else's.

Other Canadian generals, including Harry Crerar, were overeager to show what their soldiers could do in battle.

Brian Villa lays much of the blame for the fiasco at Dieppe on Lord Louis Mountbatten, Chief of Combined Operations. He titled his book on Operation Jubilee *Unauthorized Action*, and shows how Mountbatten went ahead without the approval or knowledge of any chief of staff of the armed forces.

Wars and crises bring forth heroes to offset the daily misery and suffering that pervades them. When Mountbatten took over as head of Combined Operations in April 1942, the Allies were still in dire straits. The Americans had just entered the war and had not geared up for it. The Russians had suffered huge setbacks and lost millions of men as German armies drove towards Leningrad, Moscow, and the Caucasus.

A hero was needed.

And one appeared.

Lord Louis Mountbatten—tall, handsome, of noble birth (a cousin of the king), a favourite of the Americans and of Churchill—played the role to the hilt. Richard Hough's adulatory biography of Mountbatten, subtitled "A Hero for Our Time," tells of the man's "irresistible need for self-glorification." Mountbatten believed "he had never made a single mistake in his life." Hough ascribes these personality traits to underlying feelings of insecurity: people with them must continually prove their worth to others. One historian called Mountbatten an "egregious political climber...responsible for the shambles at Dieppe."

General Montgomery called him a "very gallant sailor... Doesn't know how to fight a battle." In June 1939, Mountbatten took command of the destroyer HMS *Kelly*, and as one source put it, "his sea career was short, colourful, and unsuccessful." Within a few months, the *Kelly* had almost capsized, collided with another destroyer, been mined and torpedoed twice, and finally sunk off Crete on May 23, 1941. Mountbatten behaved heroically as the destroyer capsized, keeping up the morale of the survivors by starting a singsong, shouting "three cheers for the old ship" as the *Kelly* took its final plunge. Mountbatten's friend Noel Coward wrote the script (with David Lean), as well as directed, produced, and starred in the movie *In Which We Serve*, based on the sinking of the *Kelly*. Released in September 1942, it lifted the spirits of the embattled British, created a powerful mythology about Mountbatten, and made his role in anything he did beyond criticism. He also proved an ideal fit with Churchill's aggressive instincts and desire to keep attacking the Germans.

After the Dieppe raid, Mountbatten sent a signal to Churchill in Cairo: "Morale of returning troops reported to be excellent. All I have seen in great form." At a press conference on August 20, Mountbatten announced: "We did not accomplish all our objectives...But we did accomplish our main purpose."

The failure of the raid on Dieppe cannot be ascribed to a single individual. But many in the Canadian military still hold Mountbatten responsible for it. When he addressed a meeting in Canada, survivors of the raid walked out of the hall.

Hough writes: "To the end of his life 'Dieppe' was engraved upon Mountbatten's heart, and the name would always raise a defensive response, almost as if he were protesting too much."

The name of the French town was, and still is, engraved on the hearts of many Canadians who lost loved ones there because Mountbatten refused to cancel Operation Jubilee.

The Cost of Jubilee
The failure of the raid on Dieppe did not affect Mountbatten's reputation, and he moved on to other things. But to those

who took part in it, and their families, this military blunder left indelible impressions. Able Seaman Albert Kirby, RCNVR, expressed the feelings of other survivors of the battle when he wrote: "So relieved to be home. So happy to be in one piece... so angry that I was even part of something so confusing, agonizing, demanding and apparently unrewarding."

Mona Gould's poem, "This Was My Brother," dedicated to "Mook," Lt. Col. Howard McTaggart of the Royal Canadian Engineers, catches the quiet courage and dedication of so many others who died at Dieppe:

> *This was my brother*
> *At Dieppe,*
> *Quietly a hero*
> *Who gave his life*
> *Like a gift*
> *Withholding nothing.*

The poem ends:

> *He was awfully good at fixing things,*
> *At stepping into the breach when he was*
> *needed.*
> *That's what he did at Dieppe;*
> *He was needed.*
> *And even death must have been a little*

shamed
At his eagerness.

In nine hours, after two years of intensive training, the Second Canadian Infantry Division lost half its strength. Of the 2,211 soldiers who returned to England, half had not landed. Of those who did land, 589 had been wounded and 28 later died. Total Canadian casualties on Operation Jubilee came to just under 3,000: 58 officers and 851 other ranks killed; 1,946 taken prisoner (more than were captured by the Germans during the campaign in Northwest Europe). Of the prisoners, 554 were wounded and 71 died in captivity. Because regiments drew recruits from local communities, the disaster at Dieppe hit certain parts of Canada very hard. Practically every member of a company made up of workers at E. D. Smith's jam factory in Winnipeg lost his life. Prisoners included a brigadier and four battalion commanders. Many able officers and NCOs who could have passed on their knowledge of battle to others were lost at Dieppe.

British Army and Royal Marine casualties totaled 275; the Royal Navy lost 550 officers and ratings. The Commonwealth cemetery at Dieppe holds the remains of hundreds of Canadians killed on August 19, 1942. The savagery of the fighting is shown by the fact that 121 bodies could not be identified. The tides of the English Channel carried other dead and drowned to watery graves, during and after the battle.

German casualties came to 591: 316 in the army, 113 in the navy, 162 in the air force, and each of them, like the Canadians, was someone's son, husband, or brother. A photo shows a German funeral parade marching through an empty street, past curious children and indifferent adults, one of whom has turned his back on the procession.

Some of the survivors of Dieppe had a moment of triumph there, in September 1944. Ross Munro tells of Canadians in the Second Division moving through Rouen and heading for Dieppe. Led by a reconnaissance unit under Major Dennis Bult-Francis, who had been wounded there in 1942, the advancing troops included other survivors of the raid from the Essex Scottish, the Royals, the Rileys, and the South Saskatchewan Regiment. They expected a tough fight at the port. Bombers stood ready to raid it while warships offshore pointed their guns at the town. Canadians entered Dieppe at 1030 hours on September 1, only to find that the Germans had fled. Members of the reconnaissance unit rescued three German prisoners about to be executed by the French Resistance.

On September 3, Canadian troops marched through Dieppe in memory of, and in homage to, those who had taken part in Operation Jubilee, past sidewalks crowded with cheering French men, women, and children.

In all, 134 awards were made to participants in the raid, including a Distinguished Service Order (DSO) to Captain

An unidentified Canadian soldier, armed with a Thompson machine gun, escorting a German prisoner captured during Operation Jubilee, the Dieppe raid. England, August 19, 1942.

Whitaker, a rare medal for a junior officer. General Roberts also received a DSO for "ability, courage and determination to a high degree." However, he lost his command, was sent to train reinforcements, and concluded, "my active career was certainly finished at Dieppe."

The Plight of the Prisoners

The Germans gave their captives water and medical attention before marching them through the streets of Dieppe to be filmed and photographed for propaganda purposes. Photographs show Canadian soldiers, some in full battle-dress, others barely clad and barefoot, lined up and parading through the streets. Behind them they would have heard the sound of gunshots as Germans killed their badly wounded comrades. The Canadians retained their discipline. A German officer noted "the way they got hold of themselves and went into captivity was excellent." In one German photo, a group of captives sprawls over a field. With a cheeky grin, a Canadian soldier holds up two fingers in the "V for Victory" sign.

The wounded, sent to local hospitals, were operated on without anaesthetics. The unwounded, loaded into cattle cars, began their journey to Obermarsfeld prisoner-of-war camp. They received little sustenance from their captors who forbade French people from offering them food. Residents at L' église Saint-Martin were allowed to give them water. Several members of the FMR, including Sgt. Major Dumais, escaped from the train. Aided by their ability to speak French, they passed themselves off as Frenchmen. Dumais travelled across France, reached Marseilles, was picked up by a boat, and taken to Gibraltar. After serving in North Africa, he joined MI 9, part of British Intelligence, and returned to France. Dumais organized a very successful escape line that rescued 118 downed Allied flyers.

His comrades were much less fortunate, spending the rest of the war in captivity. Eight days after the raid, at their first prisoner-of-war camp, a British medical officer reported on their arrival: "...these people just fell out [of the cattle cars] absolutely whacked. Covered in excreta and in terrible shape. They'd been there for days...the stench, the horror, the tragedy of it all."

The misery of the survivors of Dieppe increased when the German High Command ordered that "all British officers and men captured at Dieppe shall be put in chains from 3rd September, at 2 o'clock." After being cancelled, the order was reinstated on October 8 after further study of material found at Dieppe. The British and Canadian governments responded by shackling German prisoners.

At POW camp Oflag VII B, 300 Canadian and British officers, confined in a storeroom in a nearby castle, had their wrists bound with ropes. Then they were handcuffed and tied up with metal chains from eight in the morning to nine at night. The prisoners became skilled at removing the chains as shackling became routine. Guards dumped the chains on a table. Each prisoner took a set, hung it by his bed, and put it back on the table in the evening for the guards to remove. By November 23, 1943, the shackles no longer arrived in the morning and another ordeal of the men of Dieppe ended.

Under the Geneva Convention governing the treatment of prisoners of war, officers cannot be forced to work, but other ranks can, provided what they do does not directly aid the enemy war effort. Armand Emond of the FMR spent thirty-two months in captivity, fourteen of them in handcuffs. A German guard told him: "Any prisoner who does not work will be shot." Emond worked in the woods for ten hours a day; twelve hours when harvesting grain and potatoes. The soldier reported: "Between us, as prisoners, the relationship was very solid. We were like brothers." As the Russians advanced from the east in the spring of 1945, the Germans emptied the prisoner-of-war camps in their path and sent their occupants on death marches to prevent them being captured by the "Ivans." Emond and his companions trekked through Poland and Germany for seven weeks in bitter weather, foraging for carrots and anything edible to sustain themselves. Finally they met tanks of General Patton's Third Army. Their guards threw away their weapons, shouting "*Der krieg ist fertig*" (The war is over).

The freed Canadians made their way home, scarred in body and mind, with bitter memories of the debacle at Dieppe. But, like most frontline soldiers, they got on with their lives, did not dwell on the past, and did not talk about what happened on the beaches. They had lost too many friends there.

Afterword
What Was Learned

"I don't think it was worth it."
—Arthur Rossell, aged 92, of the
Essex Scottish Regiment, on returning
to Dieppe on August 9, 2012

The Allies learned a great deal from Operation Jubilee, some of which, as already noted, should have been obvious before the raid was mounted.

It would be impossible to take a French port by storm to use as a supply base for the invading armies. All those along the French coast were heavily defended and the Germans reinforced their fortifications after the raid on Dieppe. This port had been guarded by 1,400 mediocre troops. Strongly entrenched, their quality mattered little. All they had to do was point their weapons at the Canadians on the beaches of Dieppe and open fire. A handful of German soldiers practically wiped out the Royal Regiment of Canada at Blue Beach.

If the Allies could not capture a port, they would have to take one with them. Mountbatten claimed credit for the idea of the Mulberries, huge artificial harbours towed across the Channel, sunk off the coasts of Normandy and used to transfer men and supplies to the beachhead. One was destroyed in a storm on June 19. The other carried up to 10,000 tonnes of equipment and supplies a day until December 1944. Bits of the Mulberries still lie like stranded whales off the French coast.

Another lesson identified the need for massive bombardment before soldiers landed and while they were advancing. The 4.7-inch guns of the destroyers and the bombs and cannon shells of the planes did little to suppress the rain of weapon fire directed at the landing craft and soldiers on the beach at Dieppe.

The disaster at Dieppe led to the development of specialized tanks and new machines, known as "Hobart's Funnies," after the innovative major general who devised them. They included tanks that fired petards, huge bombs known as "flying dustbins" that could obliterate enemy pillboxes, flail tanks that cleared paths through minefields, and special vehicles that laid bridges. The Americans refused to use these new inventions when they landed at Omaha Beach on D-Day. The result, as shown in the opening scenes of *Saving Private Ryan*, resembled what happened at Dieppe.

Afterword: What Was Learned

The Germans, aware that any future attack on France would come over the beaches, installed obstacles on them rather than relying simply on barbed wire. Angled pieces of iron topped with explosive charges ripped the bottoms out of landing craft, and other nasty killing and blocking devices made beach landings dangerous and difficult. Hitler exulted:

This is the first time that the British have had the courtesy to cross the sea to offer the enemy a complete sample of their weapons. We must realize that we are not alone in learning a lesson from Dieppe. The British have also learned. We must reckon with a totally different mode of attack and at quite a different place.

The Allies, realizing the shortcomings of the Churchill as a battle tank, replaced it with the Sherman. During the Dieppe raid, the invaders used the Sten gun for the first time. Although cheap to manufacture, this is not a very effective weapon, as I can report from personal experience. It can chop a finger off the user, is prone to jamming, and its bullets appear to fall out of the muzzle. The Allies kept it in production, but soldiers increasingly relied on the American Tommy gun. Like the Bren gun, it proved to be a reliable weapon.

It's impossible today to envisage what happened on the beaches of Dieppe on that tragic day so long ago. The town, a charming, lively tourist and fishing port, harbours yachts and pleasure boats. Clean, white buildings line the seafront. The town shows few signs of battle. A new casino, amusement parks, lawns, and parking lots cover land over which Canadians fought and died.

As you approach Dieppe on the ferry from Newhaven and see the white cliffs on either side of it rising above the harbour entrance and the beach, you wonder how Canada's soldiers found the courage to attack such a place. From the castle above White Beach you have a clear view of where the Canadians landed and the sea approaches. Slipping and sliding on the pebbled beach, past picnicking families and bikini-clad sunbathers, you marvel how heavily laden soldiers kept their feet as they rushed for the seawall under fire. Looking at the row of hotels and houses facing the main beach, you recognize how so many years ago those occupying them had a clear field of fire.

Whenever the story of the raid on Dieppe is told, one outstanding feature emerges: the bravery of the Canadians who took part in it. In his poem "Jubilee," Peter Taylor asks: "What is this bloody touchstone to a nation?" The answer to this question lies in the dedication that the Canadians showed to their comrades and the courage so many of them demonstrated under impossible odds.

Dieppe is Denis Whitaker and three other officers

covering the retreat of their men from the casino. Dieppe is Everett McCormick dying as he held a Bangalore torpedo in place to blow a hole through the barbed wire on top of the seawall so his comrades could advance. Dieppe is John Foote going out again and again under fire to rescue a wounded man and take him to safety. Dieppe is Cecil Merritt leading his men across the bridge at the river Scie. Dieppe is 100 lesser-known tales of how the best and the bravest of Canada's soldiers did what they could to maintain the honour of their regiments and save the lives of their comrades in the face of death.

On August 19, 1943, an editorial in *The New York Times* paid tribute to what the citizen soldiers of Canada's volunteer army had done a year earlier: "Men afoot and men in tanks were exposed to fire that no valor could withstand. Hundreds of them went as far as they could and died, but these deaths achieved nothing except to prove what was already known—the high quality of the Canadian troops." Identifying Dieppe as a spot on the French coast that will forever be sacred to the British and their allies, the editorial concluded that this was the place "where brave men died without hope for the sake of proving that there is a wrong way to invade. They will have their share of glory when the right way is tried."

Canadians should remember what their soldiers, sailors, and airmen did in this ill-conceived, ill-planned attack on an entrenched enemy. Throughout the Second World War, Canadians received the toughest assignments as the Allied armies moved towards Germany. They gained the reputation as being the best of fighters. This spirit, directed towards peaceful ends, has become a hallmark of life in Canada since 1945.

Courage, dedication, and commitment to the service of others marked the dire day of August 19, 1942. These qualities remain in abundance in Canada today as the nation struggles to deal with difficult times. Nothing that the present generation will experience can match what happened to Canadians at Dieppe. Yet many of them survived to fight another day. That's one lesson learned at Dieppe that all Canadians should remember.

Acknowledgements

The author wishes to thank Amanda Lucier and Martha Tuff for doing such a splendid job of turning my manuscript into a book, and Joan Dixon for her meticulous editing. He would also like to thank the librarians in his life without whose help he could not have put pen to paper—or finger to typewriter— to write this and his other books.

About the Author

Born in Liverpool, England, in 1929, Jim Lotz survived the blitz on the city, and then spent two inglorious years in the Royal Air Force and a year as a trader in Nigeria. Arriving in Canada in 1954, he worked as a cartographer, billing clerk, and advertising copywriter before attending McGill University. He spent two summers as a weather observer in Labrador-Ungava and four seasons with expeditions to Northern Ellesmere Island. Between 1960 and 1966, he worked for the Department of Northern Affairs and National Resources as a community planner and research officer, then spent five years teaching and carrying out research on community development at Saint Paul University in Ottawa. Between 1971 and 1973, he taught—and learned from—students at Coady International Institute at Saint Francis Xavier University. Since 1973, he has lived the freelance life, as a writer, magazine editor, association executive, and teacher. His twenty-eight published books include *Canadians at War* (Bison, 1990); *A Century of Service: Canada's Armed Forces from the Boer War to East Timor* (The Nova Scotia International Tattoo, 2000); an autobiography, *The Best Journey in the World* (Pottersfield Press, 2008); an academic work on community development, *The Lichen Factor* (UCCB Press, 1998); three northern murder mysteries; and a thriller set in the Halifax Explosion. In 2012, he received an honorary Doctorate of Civil Law from Saint Mary's University and was awarded the Queen's Jubilee Medal. In 1997, Jim visited Dieppe with his wife Pat and walked the beaches where so many brave Canadians suffered and died.

Bibliography

Bell, Ken. *The Way We Were.* Toronto: University of Toronto Press, 1988.

Bishop, Arthur. *Courage in the Air.* Toronto: McGraw-Hill Ryerson, 1992.

———. *Courage on the Battlefield.* Toronto: McGraw-Hill Ryerson, 1993.

———. *Unsung Courage 1939–1945.* Toronto: HarperCollins, 2001.

Brown, Angus, and Richard Gimlett. *In the Footsteps of the First Canadian Army: Northwest Europe 1972–1945.* Ottawa: Magic Lantern Publishing, 2009.

Churchill, Winston. *The Hinge of Fate.* Boston: Houghton-Mifflin, 1950.

Cook, Tim. *We Were Freedom; Canadian Stories from the Second World War.* Toronto: Key Porter, 2010.

Dear, I. C. B., ed. *The Oxford Companion to World War II.* Oxford: Oxford University Press, 1995.

Dumais, Lucien. *The Man Who Went Back.* London: Leo Cooper, 1975.

Eyewitness Travel. *France.* London: DK Publishing, 2010.

Flower, Desmond, and James Reeves, eds. *The Taste of Courage: The War 1939–1945.* New York: Harper and Bros, 1960.

Bibliography

Gilbert, Martin. *The Second World War*. Toronto: Stoddart, 1989.

Granatstein, J. L. *The Last Good War*. Vancouver: Douglas and McIntyre, 2005.

Granatstein, J. L., and Dean F. Oliver. *The Oxford Companion to Canadian Military History*. Don Mills: Oxford University Press, 2011.

Greenhous, Brereton. *Dieppe, Dieppe*. Montreal: Art Global, 1992.

Hough, Richard. *Mountbatten: A Hero of Our Time*. London: Weidenfeld and Nicolson, 1980.

Reader's Digest. *The Canadians at War 1939–45*. Vol. 1. Pleasantville: Reader's Digest, 1976.

Rickard, John Nelson. *The Politics of Command. Lieutenant General A.G.L. McNaughton and the Canadian Army, 1939–1943*. Toronto: University of Toronto Press, 2010.

Reynolds, Quentin. "Dress Rehearsal: The Story of Dieppe." In Reader's Digest, *Illustrated History of World War II*. Pleasantville: Reader's Digest, 1978. p. 182–189.

Roberston, Terence. *The Shame and the Glory: Dieppe*. Toronto: McClelland & Stewart, 1967.

Stacey, C. P. *The Canadian Army: 1939–1945: An Official Summary*. Ottawa: Kings Printer, 1948.

Stone, I. F. "Capital Thoughts on a Second Front." *The Nation*, October 3, 1942.

Villa, Brian. *Unauthorized Action: Mountbatten and the Dieppe Raid.* Toronto: Oxford University Press, 1989.

Whitaker, Denis and Shelagh. *Dieppe: Tragedy to Triumph.* Whitby: McGraw-Hill, 1992.

Photo Credits

Library and Archives Canada: p.12, C-014160; p.15, PA-113242 (Canadian Dept. of National Defence); p.20, C-017291; p.25, PA-113244 (Canadian Dept. of National Defence); p.29, C-017293; p.34, PA-183773 (Michael M. Dean / Canada Dept. of National Defence); p.49, PA-113245 (Capt. Frank Royal / Canada Dept. of National Defence); p.56, PA-134448 (Lieut. Ken Bell / Canada Dept. of National Defence); p.80, C-029878 (Canada Dept. of National Defence); p.89, PA-183771; p.95, PA-183773; p.105, PA-210156 (Canada Dept. of National Defence).

Index

Index